IS THIS
REALLY
REAL?

IS THIS REALLY REAL?

For permission requests or more information about this title or to order other books and/or electronic media, contact the publisher:

Paul Graham Jr.

paulgrahamJR316@gmail.com

ISBN: 979-8-9883844-0-3 (Hardcover)
ISBN: 979-8-9883844-1-0 (Paperback)

Front cover image and book design by Mandi Lynn – Stone Ridge Books

Printed in the United States of America

First printing edition 2023

IS THIS REALLY REAL?

PAUL GRAHAM JR.

CONTENTS

PREFACE

Please excuse the grammar in this book. I did not use an editor for this book. I'm sure it is far from perfect. It's been over 20 years since I last took any college course on writing. I think editors are extremely important and can be very helpful. If this was a different type of book, I would definitely utilize an editor. In fact, I think you should use an editor probably 99% of the time. This is the 1% time I would choose not to use an editor because I wanted this book to be 100% in my words in the telling of and accounting of the story.

THE UNFORTUNATE FIRST DOMINO TO FALL

I t was a chilly morning around 4am when I saw the sign that caused my whole momentum to suddenly stop while this epiphanic, somewhat magical feeling suddenly shuddered through my body, and I asked myself "Is this going to be the day?" As the day unfolded, so did the answer to my question. "Yes, today is the day."

We could tell that my mother was sick. You could see it in her eyes when she moved a certain way, she was in a lot of pain. Yet she still went to work every day. Every time that my brothers and I asked her to go to the doctor to get checked, she shrugged it off and kept going to work. The last time she had gone to get checked, she waited a few months for the appointment and when it came, it was just an introductory appointment where no real issues were discussed, and they gave her another appointment months later. She just gave up on the concept and kept living with the pain. She thinks she knew what it was. She had breast cancer about 10 years earlier and fought the battle with chemo and radiation and ended up winning the battle. In her mind, the pain she was experiencing was that the cancer had returned. She was not ready to go down the chemo/radiation battlefield again.

My father's fate was different than my mother's. Let's backtrack about 22 years prior to this chilly morning of epiphanic and magical feelings.

My father was the main income provider as my mother had focused on taking care of me and my younger twin brothers. My father's entire career revolved around cars. He was an excellent mechanic. My grandfather would rave about his ability to hear a noise and know exactly what the issue was. The dealership owner had noticed his abilities and promoted him to service manager. He now had to wear a suit to work but did not have enough money to buy any. The owner believed in him so much that he bought my father the suits for his new position. He went on to work as a service manager for a new car dealership for many years.

Almost a decade later, the economy was getting tough and at 39 years old, he was laid off. Over the next several months, he bounced around to a few different new car dealerships but with the same results. One summer morning he came home from work early and that was it. He was laid off for the final time. He now decided he was going to earn income by scouring for great deals on vehicles that had issues that he knew he could fix easily and then re-sell them for market value. He would be his own boss.

Unfortunately, this new venture only lasted about a month. I was 12 years old and in 7th grade. I stepped off the school bus like any other day except this day, was anything but typical. As I walked down the driveway towards the house, I saw that my dad was working on one of the cars he had found to fix and sell. It was cool to see my father when I first got home from school. When he worked at the dealership, it was long hours, and I wouldn't see him until almost bedtime. As I approached the car, I saw his legs coming out from across the front of the car. "Dad!" I called. As I got closer, I heard no response. "Dad!" I called again. This time I was close enough that he should hear me and respond.

When I arrived at the front of the car and was able to look all the way across the front end, I saw that he was pinned under the vehicle, he was not moving or responding to me. I felt my entire stomach drop. I felt my hands just let go of my schoolbooks and the mail I had just retrieved from the mailbox. I immediately ran into the house screaming "Dad's dead! Dad's dead!"

My mother had been working overnight shifts at a donut shop for extra income since my dad had been laid off. She was working 7 nights a week at times. She was still in the house sleeping. She heard my screams and came out of the bedroom looking half asleep. She ran to the door to see. "He is!" she yelled! That's when it really hit me that this was really happening.

It turned into a crazy, insane day. 911 was called, my father's brother, who only lived a couple houses down, was called to help. I have never seen anyone get here so fast. It was just chaos and I felt just in a daze in my own world. I watched my uncle jack up the car and try to save him. I saw the blood from his head wound. My mother urged me to go in and stay in the house, to which I obliged. I couldn't see the scene from in there, but I watched from the front window as paramedics and police flew down the driveway as they rushed to the scene. I watched as the local priest arrived. I barely knew him and I don't even know who called him. We were not frequent church attendees.

It was getting close to the time that my 7-year-old twin brothers would be getting home from school. What would we say to them? How would we even begin to tell them what happened? It was decided that the priest and I would wait for their bus and take them across the street to our neighbor's house.

After walking them over to our neighbor's house and sitting down at their kitchen table, "Your father had an accident." The priest tells them. I hear the old grandfather clock making its iconic sound. The sound has stuck with me ever since and brings me right back to that day whenever I hear it. My brothers are confused. "An accident? Is he going to be ok?" they ask – not grasping the gravity of the situation. I eventually chimed in because I wanted them to know the seriousness of what had just occurred. I tell them that Dad is dead. Just hearing myself explaining it to them just seemed surreal.

The investigation and autopsy later revealed that the accident occurred earlier in the day and that he most likely did not suffer as death resulted in seconds to minutes. He had the car jacked up on jack stands and was working on a difficult part to remove. It was unclear exactly what happened but what was clear was that the most traumatic day of my life had arrived. I can't even imagine what went through my mother's mind as she was in the house sleeping the whole time while this happened. I'm sure she carried unnecessary guilt with her. No one would ever question that there was anything she could have done. She was working 7 overnights per week during some weeks. I don't know how she had any time to be awake during the day. She never remarried or even had a boyfriend again. Even though all of us encouraged her to.

The reason this day was the most traumatic and tragic day in my life, was not only just the unexpected shock of it. But it was also that I adored my father. He was so good to us kids. He was a fun dad. He would play Teenage Mutant Ninja Turtles with us, play tag, amongst other games. He would hand build things for us like the Ninja Turtle weapons. He built me a clubhouse in the backyard. He built on an addition to it when he came across some free wood materials. Being the mechanic that he was, he found good deals on motorized recreation vehicles including a three-wheeler, four-wheeler, go cart, and a mini dirt bike. At a young age, we had all kinds of fun toys to ride. My Dad was like a big kid, he enjoyed playing with us and making us happy. When one of the vehicles broke down, he put his skills to work and would get it running again. I can't even begin to remember how many Saturdays we would spend most of the day riding in the field next to our house. My childhood was filled with so much joy, imagination, and fun activities.

He also loved fast cars and loud engines. So of course, he introduced us to New England Dragway, which was a drag racing track about 2 hours from our home. There I experienced things like feeling the heat from a jet powered engine installed in a car. I would feel the vibrations throughout my body every time they throttled the engines. It always amazed me how you could feel those things from all the way in the spectator seats. The thrilling feeling of awe watching them roar down the track at speeds approaching 300 mph. After my dad had passed, this was one of the first trips I made when I got my driver's license. He introduced me to a sport that I am still very much in love with today.

My Dad was such a happy guy. He was always laughing and joking yet had that serious work ethic side to him. He would work lake nights during the week but then on the weekends, he would be home, usually working in the yard, keeping up on his beautiful green lawn and mulch gardens. He would spend time with us whether it was riding in the field or taking us somewhere fun. He always made time for us. I don't know how he fit everything in.

The days of the wake and the funeral really showed us that it was not just us that he was a joy to be around, but many others.

There was such an outpouring of attendees at his services. The line seemed to never end. He touched so many people's lives with his happy, fun nature and selfless acts. My mother always described him with the cliché – "He would give you the shirt off of his back". I think in some ways by him dying while my brothers and I were at such young ages, he kind of became legendary in our eyes. There were so many great stories told about him. We would always be so captivated by every word whenever any of his old friends or family members would gather us around and tell the tales of the fun and sometimes crazy stories. My Dad was not afraid to live. He lived life in a way that brought joy to himself, and he shared it with others.

My father's death was a pivotal point in my life, much bigger than I even realized it would be. Just because of the chain of events that would ensue. My family was not very religious growing up. We went to a Catholic Church very minimally, maybe sometimes for major occasions like Easter, etc. I was baptized and did my first communion. After that, not much else went on with church besides weddings and funerals. We were nowhere near any type of consistent church going family. This was how it was for most of my family. But this death caused my uncle, my father's only brother, to start looking into religion a little more closely.

My uncle lived two houses down. My father and him were best friends. They saw each other often. My uncle shared my father's passion for cars – he started his own autobody shop and worked from home. This is the same uncle who my mom called that tragic day to help. He was the one that I blinked and all the sudden he was already there trying to jack up the car and save my dad.

We were all so devastated by this unexpected loss that my uncle began to ask questions. Questions like – Where is he now? Will I ever see him again? If so, how do I see him again? My uncle started going to church more regularly. He started reading the Bible more. He wanted more than anything to know if he would see his brother again.

He found himself searching for a lot of answers. He then found Grace Gospel Church. Grace Gospel Church was a fast-growing Christian Church that was very different from the Catholic Churches that we occasionally visited. They had powerful weekly messages and would teach that the grace of God would get you into heaven. They would teach that it wasn't based on your works, that it was based on the idea that Jesus died on the cross for your sins, and if you believed in him that you would be "Saved" and when you died, you would enter the Kingdom of Heaven and see other loved ones again. This was the key to what he was looking for. He would tell us that my father, even though not a religious man, did believe in God based on conversations they had over the years. Because of this, my uncle was rejuvenated that he would see my father again.

He would tell us about this church and invited us to go. I went a few times to make him happy and it was a cool place. The messages really got me to think about life overall. But I didn't totally buy in.

I was now a few years older and approaching 18 years old. I was in high school, and I loved my science classes. I struggled very much internally with this concept of God and Jesus. I truly wanted to believe, but I couldn't fully believe in it with all the science. I loved my biology classes and at one point thought of becoming a doctor. I just loved learning how things worked. Evolution was taught in my high school, and it made sense to me. I would occasionally pray to God because of my upbringing. Even though we weren't big church goers, God was talked about in our family, and this notion that he was up there somewhere.

After my father passed, various family members like my aunts, uncles, etc. were all telling me my father was in a "better place". But when I really sat alone by myself, I struggled to believe it was all real. It seemed like a fairy tale story people told themselves to be good in life. I couldn't get past the science and how the whole universe seemingly all worked together without a "God" definitely playing a role in the process. The Sun, the moon, how organisms can be born and then die, just the circle of life. Then I would contemplate, with all of these people that have died over all these years, how is there room in heaven for everyone? Where is heaven? Where is hell? No one has ever found these places while exploring the earth or space.

I really struggled with the debating inside of my head. I would be spiritually drawn to want to believe so I would see my father again. I would envision heaven and God and seeing my dad. But the logic didn't make sense to me. When I got into believing mode,

11

logic would creep in, and I would often wonder Is this really real? The answer always was maybe, but probably not. I hoped it was true, but I had no proof. And with no proof, it was tough for me to believe.

Then I would start to see some signs in life that really made me question, Is God and Jesus real? Could it really be true?

I started going through some emotional things in life. One thing I had always wanted was a girlfriend. The emotional feelings that I thought of with having that one special person in my life to connect with and to feel those butterfly feelings in my stomach, was something that I very much desired and hoped for.

But it is really much more than just butterfly feelings. It is one of the things that can bring you pure genuine happiness. I'm not even talking about love yet. I'm talking about those initial feelings you start to feel about someone after you get to know them just a little bit. Your initial feelings about someone that attracts you to them. Whether it's their natural beauty, the way they present themselves, how they do their hair, how they dress, how they conduct themselves and interact with people. Maybe it's their sense of humor, how they display their emotions, how kind and thoughtful they are, their intelligent responses and thoughts. Maybe they smile a lot and seem to be someone that enjoys life, uplifts your spirits, and puts you in a positive mood to be around.

There are so many attributes that go into being attracted to a special someone. As your brain is evaluating and processing all of these elements, you start to generate emotional feelings and thoughts that you want to get to know this person better and perhaps be in a relationship with them.

Then if you add on the thought that this person that you feel this attraction and admiration towards, also feels the same way about you - It just brings such an immediate feeling of genuine and true happiness. It gives you an exhilarating, almost euphoric feeling that resonates inside of you. It is a feeling like no other.

It gives you true inner confidence that you are someone special. But, as euphoric and mesmerizing as it feels to connect with that special person and the inner confidence that it gives you, it can have the complete opposite effect when it doesn't happen for you. When you start to feel all of those amazing feelings about someone else and they don't feel that same way about you. It can destroy your inner confidence and feelings of self-worth.

We always hear that we shouldn't base so much of our self-worthiness on another person. But the truth is, I get why we do it. I would argue that people are what bring the most genuine happiness in this life. Spending happy times with people is what is priceless on this earth. The emotions that people can make you feel are unmatched by any material thing. So, it makes sense to me that the hardest of emotional times can come from how others feel about us or treat us. That's what makes this whole thing difficult. Because people are not perfect. People make mistakes. People don't always agree with you or feel the same way as you do about certain things. It's a tricky road to travel down.

After my father had passed away, I kind of went into a shell at school. I was in 7th grade, and I became shy, and didn't talk to too many people. I was sociable before that. In my small elementary school, I even had a thing called "Paul's Club" - how original. I even made myself the president of the club and people actually joined this thing.

I slowly broke out of my shyness as high school went along and started becoming more sociable again and accumulated a group of friends. One friend I really want to mention is my friend Lenny. Thanks to him, I didn't drift off somewhere. He was one of my first friends and kept at it with me even though we were not always in the same classes anymore. He made it a point to stay in touch with me during all these things I was going through.

During this time, I was especially shy around girls. I would sometimes develop crushes on some of the popular girls and actually got the nerve to ask a couple out, but as they say I had "no game" lol. It was always the not at this time or whatever reason. I was clueless with how to interact with girls I had a crush on. There was no warming them up, just bam I'd ask the question. Looking back, no wonder I got the replies that I got. I loved sports and would play with my friends after school. But I never played on any of the high school teams. I never really got too involved in school activities which probably limited my opportunities to meet and have that special relationship with a girlfriend.

One thing about the girls in school is that I was a bit of a dreamer. I always looked up to those certain ones that just gave me those butterfly feelings. I was picky in a sense. I had no right to be, I was no Tom Cruise or Brad Pitt or whoever the heartthrob was back then. But for whatever reason I was very selective. It wasn't all about looks. I was just always looking for the total package - looks, personality, caring nature, etc. Whatever that combination was that would get my heart beating a little faster and just bring pure genuine happiness with the thought of being in a relationship with them.

One time a year or two after high school there was a girl that would come into the store I worked at and talk to me. My co-workers, knowing I had no girlfriend asked, "Paul why don't you ask her out?". I would always brush it off, but the truth was, I didn't get those butterfly feelings. Instead of just going on a date with someone and seeing how it goes, I was waiting to have those butterfly feelings after initially meeting them or seeing them for the first time so to speak. Totally limiting my chances of eventually having a great relationship by the way. When my co-worker said this to me, it really made me examine myself and ask myself. Why don't I just go out with a girl and take a chance? I realized that I would look long term and ask myself if I could see myself being married to this person, etc. I was always looking for a serious relationship and trying to plan out my future. I had so little relationship experience and pre-conceived notions that I had no idea what the heck I was doing. And thus, did not end up with a girlfriend for a couple of years and certainly not in high school.

There was one girl during the summer after I graduated high school that I did have a crush on, that I started hanging out with.

We would go to fun places together, share some laughs, it was just really a good time hanging out with her. When I told her how I felt about her, things went south. She either didn't feel that same way about me or wasn't ready for a relationship, whatever it was. I was heartbroken and then all of the other feelings came with it. "I'm never going to get a girlfriend". "What's wrong with me?". "Why am I not good enough?" - The whole "whoa is me" feelings came over me. To me writing this now seems so extreme, especially knowing now that this was not the right girl for me. But at the time they were such real feelings for me. I didn't have enough emotional experience in the world to deal with these at the time. I lived my life on the outside fine, but on the inside, I was crumbling. I felt lost. I asked my uncle about going back to his church that he had found. I started going on my own. I started going weekly. I was soul searching for answers. The further away I got from school, the further away I got from all of the science that was being taught each day. I started to pray more and talk to "God" more even though I had no idea if he was really real.

Every week I would hear a great message that really made me look at life though a different lens. Every service they would ask people that have never given their life to Christ to raise their hands while every head was bowed and every eye was closed. I could have easily slid up my hand. But I still had questions. Was this really real? I still had science on my brain and thought the world made logical sense without God.

Months would go by, and I wouldn't raise my hand. I wasn't

truly in. But then one day they had someone singing songs before the message. One song was about Jesus and how he was walking in the streets, and it just painted a real picture in my head. I felt like I was there in the streets and watching Jesus. I felt Jesus was a real person. I let go of the science and logic for a minute. It was like an epiphany that hit me like a ton of bricks that this was all real. So that day I decided to raise my hand and take a leap of faith and truly believe that Jesus was real.

The doubts did creep in again as years went by but there have been some signs that I have seen that have given me reason to believe that it is really real. I'm not in any way saying I have seen heaven or Jesus or God or anything like that. I'm just a guy that for whatever reason has noticed some signs. I don't even expect you to totally believe me. I would be skeptical of someone who claimed to have seen these signs if I didn't see them myself. And for that fact I've even questioned myself on even writing this book. But I've seen enough signs to say that I feel like I have to share this with others. It's just been too many signs to just be coincidences. Too often, I've picked up on these little signs that have caused me to feel a sudden epiphanic sensation of awe and amazement, almost euphoric with a magical touch. Each one would cause me to stop for a moment, just smile, shake my head, look up and say, wow, that's crazy!

CHAPTER 1
My Hero

S o back to that chilly morning at 4am that I began telling at the very beginning of the book. I was a covering store manager at Cumberland Farms. It was November in New England. It was dark. It was cold. I had just arrived to open the store for the day. The night before I was at my mother's house. She was on hospice. She had been diagnosed with stage 4 lung cancer. Close family members were there. The hospice nurse met with us and told us that my mother shouldn't be left alone anymore, that we should be on shifts to care for her. Her condition was definitely worsening. She was on a lot of pain meds and was barely awake nor herself. To me, I knew it would be a matter of weeks at the most before we lost "mom".

I was so proud that my mother was my mother. After what happened to my father, She stepped up even more. She had 3 boys. She hadn't had a career going because she was a stay-at-home mom until she started working overnights shits at the donut shop for extra money for the house. She was a very smart woman who did excellent in school and could have been very successful if she was career driven. But she was family driven. And that's how it was in a lot of households in the 80's.

After my father's tragedy, she now in an instant had to raise 3 boys on her own, cope with her grief as she had just lost her husband on top of also losing her mother and father the year prior, coping with losing all three in a 1-year span. She had to figure out how to pay the mortgage and take care of everything. At 12 years old, I didn't totally get it. But as you go through life, there is no one I learned to appreciate more for their sacrifices than my mother. She was the most selfless person that I have ever known. She put all of our needs before her own. There was never a Christmas where we didn't feel like we didn't get the main things we asked for. We never went without new clothes for school each year. We never went without food on the table. We never went without a roof over our heads as she managed to keep paying the mortgage and keep the home we had grown up in. I don't know how the heck she did it. But she did. Once maturity set it on my part and I realized all that she had done for us, my hero was born.

One positive thing that came from losing our father at young ages is that it brought our family closer together. Not that we weren't close before that, but enduring that tragedy and being raised by a single mother brought all of us closer. My brothers and I developed very strong bonds in life. We always try to have each other's back in life. They were co-best men at my wedding. I could never choose one over the other. Each one I have a unique bond with, whether it's our love for cars and going to the Dragway or if it's talking sports and catching a game together. As we each got older, the more all of our interests mixed together and all three of us now get together for the same events. Our mother's love and ability to withstand hardship was the glue to our relationships.

My mom always displayed so much love. She was easy to talk to. Whenever anything great happened in my life, my first thought would be to call my mom. When I was down, I would talk to my mom. Although I would never tell her everything, for some reason there were certain things I just felt like I couldn't tell anyone. I would only talk to God about them when I prayed. There are always those things that we feel embarrassed that we feel that way about something and we just don't feel comfortable telling someone else because of fear that they will not understand exactly how we are feeling or might judge you. As nice and loving as my mom or someone is, sometimes I still feared telling them. But I never felt fear when talking to God whether it was when I believed in him or wasn't totally sure he was real. One thing was certain. I always felt comfortable quietly talking to him in my head when I needed someone to hear my feelings.

I don't know how my mother did what she did. I really don't.

She was the best mother a son could ever ask for. She went through so much for her children. She endured so many hardships in life and kept going. That's why it was so tough to see her so sick. The initial signs started to become more and more obvious.

Besides noticing her wincing in pain before the hospice and while she was still working, another thing that made me realize it was time for her to get checked was when I came to her house one day. I noticed her sink was full of dirty dishes. I opened the fridge, and she had McDonald's bags in the fridge. This was a woman who always had a clean house and kept up on the dishes. She always cooked meals, big meals all the time for us when we were growing up. As much as she tried to say everything was fine and not to worry. I knew it was anything but.

Soon after seeing the dirty dishes, I was at my doctor's appointment. I mentioned to him about my mother. She was not feeling well. We could all tell. We knew that she had the feeling that the cancer had returned. I told him that we consistently tell her to get checked. She puts it off. I explained to him that when she did actually take the time and made an appointment, she got the run around and after waiting for the first appointment, and that after she went to it, they didn't do much. They told her it was more of a "consultation" and just made her make a second appointment, which she just never ended up going to.

I asked my doctor if he could see her soon and assess her in that one appointment. He agreed. I got the appointment card, and I immediately went to my mother's work. I gave her the card and said "Mom, I set everything up. I explained to the doctor what happened to you last time and that you just want one appointment. I'll go with you" I thought she was going to fight it, but she said, "Thank you Paul, I'll go".

So, we went to the appointment, and she got evaluated. The doctor suspected lung cancer. She agreed to go see a specialist and get some tests done. It didn't take too long for these appointments and devastatingly, lung cancer is what it ended up being. Stage 4. She was given 6 months or so to live. We knew she was sick. We could see the pain in her eyes. She had been going to work every day like this. I couldn't fathom how she was doing it physically and mentally.

After the diagnosis, she told her work employer and went on a leave of absence. There was one different thing this time around with the cancer. She was mentally drained. She had done the chemo and radiation the last time. She knew she didn't want to go through that again. Here she was less than 2 months from her 60th birthday and she was given 6 months to live. Obviously, some family members urged her to go through the treatment and fight it. But I could see in her eyes that she was done fighting at least to the level that she knew this battle would take. She just wanted to enjoy as much as she could of her final months/days. She didn't want all of the side effects that the treatment would bring.

I told her that I wanted her to fight it but that I also understood that she already knows what it's like to go through that treatment. So, if she decided that she did not want to fight it, that I would understand and support her decision.

She was still "Mom" and fully alert but with the diagnosis we helped her research and she decided to get hospice involved. It was September when she was diagnosed and stopped working. She stayed home. She started her pain meds and had hospice checking in on her. We would stop by frequently to check in on her and if there was anything she needed. She was still very self-sufficient. She was very controlling too, she made sure that she herself counted out her meds and took the proper doses. She wrote it down on a log sheet she made.

The family was notified, and we planned for them all to celebrate with her on her 60th birthday the following month. By this time, she was not nearly herself. She laid down most of the day. She could have conversations but would sleep a lot with the medications. It was great that so many of her family members got to be there and visit her on her birthday. It was a very emotional night just seeing everyone. The feeling was that it was the last time some of her family would see her. Her brother flew out from Arizona to be there. She was well loved, and it showed that night.

This was such an emotional time period for me and I'm sure for everyone that loved her. To see our "Mom" just go from working a full-time job but in pain, to less than 2 months later just being a shell of herself. We watched her slowly deteriorate right before our eyes. It was such a dramatic difference between watching my mom go through this versus re-visiting my dad's tragic day. I often contemplate what is worse. Is it to lose someone you love unexpectedly and the shock of it all? Or is it to watch someone you love to go through this slow process getting worse and worse? The answer is: Both suck. There are positives and negatives to both angles of it. In one aspect you get the opportunity to tell someone everything you wanted to tell them before they go. But on the other hand, to watch someone you know suffer and slowly get weaker and weaker is pretty painful to watch.

So back to the night before the chilly morning I have been referencing since the opening of this book. We were all at the house discussing options with hospice. The nurse suggested that we should each take shifts to be with my mom. We were trying to figure out how to do this as we all had jobs. My aunt, the wife of my father's brother, I have to say was like a God sent angel during all of this. She spent so much time and was so helpful stopping by to visit my mom during the time that she was home on hospice. Her love and support were just unbelievable during this time. So, as we are deciding who can do which shifts, she offers to do some shifts, which just melted our hearts as we knew it was her children's responsibility. That night we decided on a schedule for at least the next day or two but after that we would have to figure it out. We knew she had weeks at most left. My wife decided to take the first overnight shift and stayed that night. Before I left, I hugged my mother and told her I loved her. She was barely awake. As I left towards the house door, I heard her from the other room say, "I love you Paul". I don't even know how she got enough energy to get that one off, but I felt good knowing my mom was still in there and had some alertness.

I went home to sleep and then woke up early the next morning for work. I arrived at the gas station/convenience store I worked at around 4am the next morning on this cold November day. At Cumberland Farms, one of the store manager's responsibilities was getting the competitors' gas prices and entering them into the system. It was one of the first processes to open the store. We would then get notified via the system if we had to complete a gas price change. They didn't necessarily match the competitor. They just kept the gas price in line with the market.

So, on this chilly November morning. I get the price change. I go outside, it's still cold and dark at 4am. This store was older and still had the magnetic signs that I had to put the numbers on manually. As I'm changing the numbers when it suddenly awakens me almost like a euphoric moment that the new gas price is $3.16. That's when the sudden epiphanic feeling of awe came over my body and I asked myself "Is today going to be the day?" My mother was still somewhat alert the night prior so I logically didn't think it would definitely be the day but when I changed the price of the gas to $3.16 it made me ponder it a little more.

You see John 3:16 is a Bible Verse: "For God so loved the world that he gave his only begotten Son, that whosoever believeth in Him should not perish but have everlasting life." It is the verse that the whole Gospel that was taught at the church my uncle introduced me to was based on. I had two other 3:16 moments in my life prior to this one that I will get into later on in the book. So, because of those, this stood out to me and made me ponder for a minute. I wasn't totally sure today would be the day, but I thought to myself "Wow. that would be kind of crazy if today ended up being the day". The thought of it sent a chill up my spine.

I went back inside to work and went about my day, hoping it was not the day because you are never ready to lose your loved ones, especially your loving mother. But I also had a thought that if it was the day, it would be quite the coincidence that it was the same exact day I changed the price to $3.16. Almost like a sign from her that don't worry, I'm going to be ok. I also on some level would be ok if it was the day because of all of the suffering she was going through.

Of course, I got the phone call around 12 noon from my wife and I already kind of knew. Today was the day. It was one of the most difficult times in my life. As ready as I thought I was to hear this news, you are truly never ready. The emotions rush in. My heart was broken. I wept as I drove home to see her and my family.

The devastation and grief were obvious. But also, everything else that would come over the coming days. Having to plan out a funeral with my brothers for our mother. Attending the service, just dealing with everything. Everything that my mother had to deal with when my father passed away. This was the first time I was on this end of it, having to make plans with funeral directors, pick out a casket, prayer cards, just everything that comes with a funeral service.

I have to say the services were beautiful. We gave speeches which I really was thankful for that I was able to express my feelings and share with everyone in attendance how great of a mother and woman she was. But they didn't need me to tell them. Just as my father's funeral services had a never-ending line of people, so did my mother's. I honestly don't even recall whose line was longer – but one thing was certain – both of my parents impacted a lot of lives in a positive way, and we received so much love and support during this timeframe.

On the day of the funeral there was another little sign, literally, as the hearse drove by the local Cumberland Farms gas station and the gas price here was the same that it was at the store that I worked at which was almost an hour away - $3.16. It could have easily been a different price being so far away and so many days later as gas changes prices so often. It could have easily been $3.17 or $3.15. But it was not. It was $3.16. It was just a little reminder to me, not to worry about my mom. She was ok.

CHAPTER 2
The First Sign

The first sign I received was a couple years after high school. It was during one of my lowest periods in life. It was during the timeframe when I just couldn't seem to get a girlfriend. I attached so much of my self-worth to how girls with whom I had hoped for a relationship with, viewed me. The value I placed on having one of those special relationships increased the stakes for me. Aside from the genuine happiness that would occur, finding "the one" was the start to my future of hopefully having a family one day. I wanted to give to my future children the great childhood that my parents gave me. I wanted to pass along their memories and our family traditions. I wanted to share all of the passions that I had with children of my own someday. So many life dreams that I had were attached to this one aspect of having that special relationship that may turn into marriage one day.

When it didn't work out time after time after time, my inner confidence had eroded. I felt like a loser. I felt useless. I felt like I wasn't good enough. I was just processing thoughts in a very negative light and not seeing the positives in life. It became emotionally painful. Outwardly, I was totally fine. I was outgoing still, went to work every day. I never wanted to let on that things were so bad in my mind. I had a very rough patch where I contemplated suicide often. I started to make a game plan. I purchased the supplies I would need. I started writing a journal of my thoughts so people would understand what I was going through. I told no one what I was thinking or planning. I finally hit the lowest of lows mentally one night where something really upset me, and I told myself that's it. Tomorrow is the day that I will do it. I can't take this life anymore. I just want the mental pain to end.

Now keep in mind this is after I had been going to church and got "saved" so to speak. I still had these very negative thoughts. Just because I was going to church occasionally and learning spiritually didn't mean I wasn't struggling mentally with some of these thoughts.

So, I make the decision that night that the next day will be the day. This was the final straw. I was done. I immediately felt a calm come over me because I know tomorrow it will be over. I go to sleep and the next thing I know my mom is waking me up and telling me work is on the phone. It's early in the morning and they are asking me to come in on my day off, they tell me someone called out. Me being half asleep, instinctively I say, "Yes I'll be in".

As I get ready for work, I immediately still tell myself today will still be the day, I'll do it after work. So, I'm in a pretty good mood with this thought and I go to work. I'm working my regular shift and interacting with everyone like it's a great day. I'm still depressed inside but also relieved. I'm working as a customer service representative at a Cumberland Farms gas station convenience store by the way. The same one I'm ironically just thinking about that fact now, that the hearse drives by 20 years later for my mother's funeral where the gas price was $3.16. Well, the gas price is nothing close to that on this day, all these year's prior, It's probably more like $1.16 or something.

So anyway, we have this one customer who loves Jesus and would frequently shop at the store. He would especially talk to one of my miserable co-workers who outwardly would say how much he hated the world and life. This is how I learned that this customer loved Jesus because he would try to cheer this negative co-worker up and would tell him that "Ever since I accepted Jesus as my personal lord and savior, I've been so happy in life". That co-worker has long left the company, but the customer still shops at the store.

So, I'm still just going about my day waiting for my shift to end so I can go get on with this plan. I'm looking at the cash registers, thinking this will be the last time I run this register. As I see people, I think this will be the last time I see this person. It gets slow, and I start looking off into space at the register area. I'm just in a daze thinking about the negatives in my life and the big decision I've just made. And then a customer comes to my register. As I look up, before I even make eye contact, I see his T-shirt. It's a John 3:16 bible shirt with the whole verse on there. My eyes are just stuck on his shirt like glue as I read the verse on his shirt. I've heard the verse at church, I know what it is, but I just read the shirt and it jumped out at me this day. It's like a switch went on. I'm in the moment of thinking about ending my life and then I read this verse of having eternal life by believing in Jesus. In my head, I'm just like "Wow! Is this really real?" It almost had a magical feel to it. Of course, I look up and it's that Jesus loving customer in his ever so cheery mood. We talk quick, he goes on his way.

But the thoughts after reading his t-shirt stay with me. Here I am, planning out a suicide, went to a store a few weeks ago, bought all the supplies. Finally, I had a decision-making moment to follow through with it. Today is going to be the day and what happens? I get interrupted by getting called into work. I see this 3:16 bible shirt that I couldn't stop thinking about. I couldn't shake the timing of it. I just keep re-saying the verse in my head. It starts to make me re-consider the whole thing. I start to believe again that maybe this is really real and maybe I should take more time to think about it. My mood improves as I interact with customers and co-workers. I feel better about myself. I end up changing my mind altogether. I tell myself this is crazy that on this day, I see this 3:16 shirt that I never would have seen if I didn't get called into work and who knows what I would have done that day if I didn't go to work. Would I have actually done it? I guess I don't know for sure. But I sure felt like I was in the mindset that it was going to be the day. I made up my mind and was at peace with the decision.

That moment changed my life forever. It has stuck with me ever since. It was my first 3:16 sign and I wouldn't get another one for many, many years later. It just got me back on track with believing in God and Jesus.

CHAPTER 3
My Father-In-Law

So, let's jump ahead in time. I end up meeting my eventual spouse. We met at a nightclub. She immediately caught my eye right away. I had never seen her before. What probably helped my confidence to approach her was that she was there with a somewhat mutual friend. I'm out there on the dance floor, I look over at her and I tell her that she's the most beautiful girl here. She probably just looks at me as this drunk guy that says that to everyone. But I really meant it. I was "wowed" by her beauty.

It started some brief conversations in the noisy night club. But during those conversations, she seemed sweet, nice, intelligent to talk to, always smiling. I was already feeling those "butterfly feelings". I was definitely interested in getting to know her better.

I don't think I believed I had a chance with this girl, but what helped me out was my connection to that somewhat mutual friend as that girl was friends with some of my friends and also used to shop at the convenience store when I worked there. So, after that night, I felt comfortable enough asking the girl I knew "who's your friend?" And I kept persisting that we all hang out sometime. It's funny, you never know where you're going to meet that person that changes your life forever.

The friends I met at that Cumberland Farms convenience store ended up becoming lifelong friends. As crazy as that sounds, of all the places I've worked at, that that store was the one that produced so many friendships. Ironically that's the same store of the 3:16 bible shirt incident along with what I previously mentioned of seeing the $3.16 gas price as the funeral procession for my mom drove by. I guess that little store has had quite the impact on my life.

By meeting my group of friends there, I started to get my confidence with girls. I started getting out more. We went to night clubs. It was my early 20's. We had a lot of fun and crazy nights. They also introduced me to the AOL chat rooms and online dating was just starting with things like match.com, etc. I met some girls, went on dates. No long-term relationships really.

That all began to change that night at the club when I first saw my eventual spouse. All of the stars finally aligned. All the negative experiences that I had were all part of the growing and learning process. I learned from mistakes that I had made. Each one was a building block going towards my best relationship that was about to come.

But one of the lessons that I learned and now had to apply, was to have some patience, and see how things go. Once I got the phone number for the most beautiful girl there, we ended up becoming great friends and dated at times. It was kind of a mixed friendship/relationship over the next couple of years but mostly friendship. It didn't turn into this magical relationship overnight. There was chemistry there, but other factors played a role with the timing of how it eventually worked out.

There were so many qualities that drew us together – especially the more we got to know each other. It wasn't just her external beauty that pulled me right in, it was her genuine happy smile, her caring nature, her thoughtfulness and appreciative attitude after dinner or a movie. She always said thank you and meant it. We had so many things in common like horror movies and going to theme parks or fun activities. We both just really loved to live life to the fullest. But it wasn't just living life to the fullest. It became living life to the fullest together. There was no one else I wanted to be with. She was the "one". We eventually moved in together as "friends", but we moved out of that apartment a few years later as husband and wife!

Her father was quite the character. He was definitely a little bit different than anyone I have ever met. His sense of humor, the way he interacted with people was one of a kind. Let me explain. He would love to make up crazy stories that were not true about something not that important so that you believe him. Then you would hear later on from someone else that he was just messing with you. He did this to me on many occasions in the early days and I would go along with his stories thinking they were true, having full conversations about them only to learn later on that he totally made them up. He was always so serious in the story telling. Once I was around the family more, I saw through the stories more and began to differentiate between a real story or made-up story...somewhat, he was good at it, ha-ha.

What made it interesting is after a few years and I got to know him more, my sister-in-law would bring a new date to the family cookouts or gatherings. I would sit there and watch my father-in-law do the same thing he used to do to me to others. I would just laugh inside my head so as to not give anything away. I would watch their reaction as my father-in-law would tell them some crazy story. I would watch them seemingly fully believe and engage in the made-up story. It was just one of the fun things that my father-in-law did to entertain himself.

He also liked to just take my wife's phone for example and dial a random person in her contacts and then hand it to my wife and say "Your Aunt (or whoever he dialed) wants to talk to you. My wife would take the phone and her aunt or whoever he dialed, was actually on the other line saying "Hello, Hello". He liked to play little pranks and do these little fun things.

Unfortunately, he ended up being diagnosed with cancer and ended up passing away. This was about 4 years after my wife and

I got married, and about 3 years before I would lose my mother to the same bad disease. What always stood out to me was his involvement at his local church. His wife and him would attend regularly and volunteered there. I remember some days they had security duty and had to lock up the church after service. My mother-in-law told me that he was never big into church before they met but liked the one that she went to. It was the church my wife attended before we met. My wife and I would bounce back and forth between this church and the church that I got involved with that my uncle introduced me to until we eventually switched to the church we go to now.

We went through phases in life where we would go to church often and then sometimes life would get busy, and we would not go for a while. The major holidays like Easter, etc. we would typically go to my wife's family church. They were two totally different style churches, but both had Christian roots. That was something that was important to me when I met my wife. Us both believing in God was very important to each of us.

What stood out to me and even to the Pastor there, was my father-in-law's positive attitude and calmness after his diagnosis. He would often go in the church and talk to God. He seemed very close to God. When the pastor asked him one time why he was so calm, my father-in-law replied that it was because he knew where he was going, and he was at peace with it.

One of the fun things he did while he was going through his treatment that I remember was when we were in the elevator. My wife had given him a talking Jesus doll as a gift since he liked to talk to Jesus. So here we are in the elevator with a bunch of strangers and it's so quiet you could hear a pin drop. But of course, what does my practical joker father-in-law do, even in the condition that he was in and now sitting in a wheelchair? He presses the button on the Jesus doll. So, all of the sudden from the silence, everyone hears "I am Jesus. I am the Son of God" Everyone in the elevator starts looking around like what the heck? Once we all realized what had happened, it was just a very fun comical moment that lightened the mood of what was going on. That was his personality.

My father-in-law wanted to be at home for his end days. So, he went on hospice. I remember visiting him the last day or two. He couldn't talk anymore at this time. My mother-in-law continued to play the CD that he loved hoping the music would make him feel a little better. One song that was played over and over was "Only Time" by Enya. It was a nice soothing song but also made us sad because it made us think of him lying there, knowing the end was very near.

After my father-in-law passed, it was a tough time for the family. My wife was heartbroken. He was truly missed and still is today.

Almost 2 years later, I was at work. I was newly hired as a store manager in training at Cumberland Farms. I was back at the company I started my working life with after high school. I was conducting the opening procedures in the early morning, and

I'll never forget this. I was all alone in the store, doing my work, listening to the store radio station. Then that song "Only Time" by Enya came on. This is a song I rarely, if ever, would hear on the work radio station. I immediately started thinking about my father-in-law and that whole depressing time period at the end when we continuously played this song for him. It actually makes me pause for moment. I forget where I'm at for a few seconds when the song first comes on, but then I get back into reality mode of work opening procedures.

The song is still playing and I'm in the middle of filling out paperwork for the lottery tickets for the day and I need to put today's date on it. I didn't remember what the date was, so I looked at the clock near the register and then "Wow!", I think to myself. The date was 3/16. I immediately just felt a magical, awe-like feeling. I shook my head. I was like wow, during this song is when I randomly look to find the date and I see 3/16. This was before the whole gas price change for my mom which would come the following year. At the time this was the second 3:16 sign that I had seen. It had been over 10 years since I first saw the 3:16 verse on that t-shirt on that pivotal day in my life. But seeing that T-shirt on that particular day was still etched in my memory. The significance of seeing those numbers still resonated with me all those years later. To see the numbers again at this new moment, to me it just felt like a little sign from my father-in-law, telling me that everything is ok, and he is up there.

Prior to this, I didn't really tell anyone about 3:16 signs or anything like that. I thought people would think I'm crazy. But because this had to do with my father-in-law, I felt like I should tell my wife about this one. Whether she would think I'm crazy or not or just a mere coincidence, I figured I would tell her what happened and maybe provide some comfort to her that perhaps he really is up there in a better place like we all hoped. Maybe there is some truth to this Gospel thing.

CHAPTER 4
The House

So fast forward to after my mother's death. At this time, I had now seen three 3:16 signs at very coincidental moments in my life. Could they really be signs or just coincidences? I guess it's up to what you believe. After what happens in this chapter It was really getting momentum with me that these were more than just coincidences.

Before my mother had passed away, she told us about her wishes on how she wanted her house handled. In a nutshell, she wanted one of her three sons to get the house at a very reasonable, below market rate. She knew it needed a lot of repairs that she had been unable to afford. There was still a mortgage on the house but nothing too crazy. She wanted whichever son that wanted the house to take out a reasonable mortgage to pay off the existing mortgage plus pay the other 2 brothers a lump sum each that she had determined was fair.

After trying to get on with our normal lives after our mother's death, my brothers and I started talking about the house. We had open discussions with each other about who was interested in owning and living in the house and who wasn't. Two of us were interested and one was not. We all decided that the two brothers that were interested would go to a loan officer and whoever he said was most currently qualified to afford the home would get the home and we all agreed we would stick with this decision. The last thing we wanted was anyone to feel like we all weren't in agreement with everything. We also valued what my mother's wishes were.

Part of the reason that keeping the house in the family was important to us was that there was a little bit of history with the house. It all started back in the 1950's when my grandfather owned a small farm. He eventually stopped using the land as a farm and gifted land on each side of his home to each of his two sons. From what I know, he gave comparable monetary value to his third child, his daughter.

So that's how my father and my uncle were able to live 2 houses apart and thus helping them stay close in their relationship. A lot of my childhood was spent at my uncle's house. It was a relatively quick walk through my grandfather's property. His daughter, my cousin, was about 2 years older than me and we became very close.

We played together often. The field that we used to ride our three-wheeler and go-cart, etc. was right there on my grandfather's property - very convenient and safe to get to for us children.

I was 4 years old and about to turn 5 when my parents had our home built. Most of my childhood memories were there and all of my younger brothers' childhoods were at this home. There were a lot of happy and fun memories. Memories of our dad from years prior. Memories of our family life, playing in the swimming pool, playing in the yard, and in the house itself. In a sad way, it is also the home where both of my parents unfortunately breathed their last breaths at. There was just so much history at the home, which was one of the reasons that I was interested in purchasing the home. And that is exactly what happened. My wife and I were told by the loan officer that we were in the best position at the time to purchase the home, so it was agreed that we would purchase the home.

This was also very beneficial to everyone as we had been splitting between the three of us, all of her home's utilities, mortgage payments, etc. to maintain the empty home. Now this would alleviate the burden the three of us faced of paying our share towards maintaining the empty home on top of us each paying our own individual housing payments.

Some issues arose with the purchasing of the home. First was the whole probate issue. My mother did have a Will, but unfortunately everything still had to go through probate court. Then I was starting the process of changing careers. I had been in retail most of my working life. At the beginning, I was going to college part time but then once I started making some decent money in my world, I never finished going.

Right after high school, I worked at Cumberland Farms part time. That is where I met those lifelong friends and had that first 3:16 moment. Then a new Wal-Mart was being built in my town and a couple employees had left and went there. So, after a frustrating workday, I decided to apply. They had a hiring center as the store was not ready yet. After a couple of interviews, I was hired as an Inventory Control Specialist which was just a fancy title for stocking the shelves and keeping up on backroom organization. There were other job functions, but those were the main ones.

I saw the big operation of this big box store as being much different than what I was used to in the smaller Cumberland Farms. I saw possibilities to move up with this company. There were so many different positions and levels of management. I didn't really know anyone except for those couple of other brand-new hires from Cumberland Farms. I decided to put my head down, go to work and see what happens. I was even further motivated when the district manager came in and had a store meeting with the associates. One thing he mentioned is that store managers made $150,000 - $200,000. I was a 22-year-old kid in the early 2000's and thought wow, that's a lot of money. After being there for a couple of months, I stood out enough to be selected as the store's first Inventory Control Specialist Team Leader.

Wow, I already was a supervisor. Granted it was only over five individuals or so, but hey it was something. I concentrated more on this career and slowly put college on the back burner.

I kept working hard and moving up the management ladder in the store. I went to Support Manager then to Assistant Manager after about 2½ years of being there. The Assistant Manager position was the big jump. It was like a $50,000 salary or something like that back then. But it required attending a whole training program, and I could be placed anywhere in the district once completing it.

Each store had about 5-8 Assistant Managers depending on its size. The Assistant Managers would each have an area of the store that they managed. They would oversee all of the Department Managers and Associates in that area of the store. They would conduct the interviews for hiring candidates, promoting candidates, they would do the scheduling, they would hold associates accountable, terminate associates if necessary. You had a lot of operational responsibilities and merchandising responsibilities making sure your assigned area was always in stock, neat, clean, and organized and daily tasks were completed. There was a lot to that position, much more than I mentioned, but I don't want to bore you with every detail of the job. You were pretty much like a mini store manager over your assigned area and the store manager would rotate your position every 6 months or a year so that you could learn to operate each area of the store. You would also be rotated between different stores throughout the district.

It was a lot of hours and was all salary. Whenever they asked you to come in extra, there was no extra pay. I worked for Wal-Mart for over 10 years. I learned a great deal. I eventually made it to Co-Manager, which some of the bigger stores had as a position. It was a position that was in between Assistant Manager and Store Manager. It was in essence a Store Manager in training but with additional responsibilities. I was very proud of that moment because the competition was fierce. When a Co-Manager position opened up in a district, each district had about 50 Assistant Managers. The majority of them wanted to move up in the company. There would also be candidates from other districts applying. You had to stand out as the number 1 candidate. One of the Assistants I worked under when I first started did eventually make it to Store Manager. He told me once that the odds of getting struck by lightning were better than working your way up to Store Manager. Whether he was correct or not in his mathematical analysis, one point was certain – the odds were against you.

I then started thinking about family. My wife and I wanted to start a family and had been trying for several years. I really started thinking that I wanted to be at my hopefully eventual children's soccer games or baseball games, football games, whatever it was that they wanted to do. Being in retail, the demanding schedule made that difficult. I was working at a store that was an hour from my house and started working some just insane hours every week where it really started to affect my health. My health combined with thoughts of a career change with a better work/life balance shaped my decision.

I reached out to some of my friends whom I worked with at Cumberland Farms all those years ago who stayed with the company and were now store managers. They started telling me about the benefits of the store manager position there. It was Monday through Friday, first shift, holidays off. In retail management, that is unheard of. What also inspired me was that the same Regional Managers, Loss Prevention Manager, etc. were all still there from when I was there over 10 years prior. At Wal-Mart that would be highly unlikely as high management positions would frequently turnover. This made me feel like this company treated their employees at a high level because so many were still there. Now it was going to be a dramatic pay cut for me to take on this Store Manager role, which sounds crazy because in title it's a step up, but in theory it actually seemed to be less of a responsibility because the store is much smaller.

For the betterment of my health and better work/life balance I decided to leave Wal-Mart and apply for Cumberland Farms. I interviewed and was offered the Store Manager in Training position. Even with the dramatic pay cut, I felt this was the right move going forward.

I enjoyed my time there, mostly as the company did treat its employees pretty good overall. I covered stores here and there throughout the district until a store manager position opened and then I was placed in my own store. It was during my tenure there that I saw the 3:16 signs for my father-in-law with the song on the radio and then for my mother with the gas price change that fateful day - just to place everything with time continuity.

After my mother had passed and we were dealing with all of her personal belongings, the house, etc. I started to look at life differently. I started to realize even more that I'm not getting any younger. I'm eventually going to be what her age was before she passed – 60. What am I going to do about retirement, etc? What is my life going to look like?

So, I started asking my brother, who had worked at a jail, some questions about his correction officer position. A jail was the last place I ever thought I would work and never had any interest in it. But it always seemed that my brother was on vacation or had some time off. The base schedule is only 40 hours a week. I had been in retail for so long doing 50+ hours all the time for salary, that the 40-hour work week appealed to me. So, I reached out to him to ask him about vacation time, etc. I liked what I was hearing about the 4 vacation weeks you get after one year, earning additional weeks every 5 years or so going all the way up to 7 weeks. Then there was the retirement pension where you would get 50% of your pay after 20 years of service. So, I just did quick math with let's say the rate at the time I applied, the annual pay was $50,000. Obviously in 20 years it would be much higher than that. But just for simple math purposes. If your rate was $50,000, you would be paid $25,000 every year in pension pay after you retired. So, in just 4 years of retirement, you would receive $100,000. Based on the contributions I was making into my 401K at Cumberland

Farms, it would take a lot just to reach $100,000. So, to me this part was a no-brainer.

The other part of the equation was that Retail Management was starting to get old for me. I had been doing it for so long and putting in so many long hours. It was a very busy work schedule where you never felt like you had enough hours in the day to complete everything and were always running around with a sense of urgency. Now don't get me wrong, some of that is what I actually liked about the job, but it can get old after a while. Perhaps the biggest difference with a big box store like Walmart vs smaller Cumberland Farms is that you had many more associates at Walmart. If people called out, you could slide people around. At Cumberland Farms, one call out was a big deal. You had to find someone to cover that shift and if you couldn't, you as the manager would have to cover it. So, if you have a staffing crisis, you are living at your store, don't plan on going home much. I didn't like the fact of being on call all the time. I didn't mind being on call to answer questions, but being on call to have to leave what you are doing to cover a shift, I didn't like that part. Especially since you already put in your normal 50 hours for your own mandatory schedule.

One time, I was at my best friend's wedding, and I was getting a call to come in from someone calling out. On Thanksgiving, I would be preparing a meal and would be getting a call to cover a shift. That part of it made me realize I was ready to move on. You always had that thought in the back of your mind, you could get interrupted in your personal time at any time, to have to cover a shift.

So, with all of that said, I decided to take the plunge and apply at the jail my brother worked at. It was completely different from anything I had ever done before. It was a long hiring process, it took months. It included fingerprints, a background check, interviews, etc. They would hire every correction officer at the same time and conduct a 6-week training academy to complete which included PT and classroom. It was a lot of hands on training with handcuffing and defensive tactics. It included getting sprayed in the face with pepper spray and then having to complete a drill of handcuffing while dealing with the exposure to the pepper spray. It was like no other job that I had been a part of. It was not the hardest thing I ever did in my life, but I was proud when I graduated from the academy and received my uniform.

So as far as the story of my mom's house goes, this was the point in life that I was at. I had left Cumberland Farms and began working at the jail. Now the courts were still processing the probate paperwork, so we couldn't do anything official with the house as of this point anyway, but this job change would push it back one year later as I had to be in the same field of employment for at least one year.

My wife and I had already moved into my mother's house and just took over the monthly bills so as to unburden all of us with keeping up on the empty house. After the first year went by at my new correction officer job and the probate finished, it was finally time to apply for the mortgage and finalize the house. It was exciting times as we had always rented in the past. We were finally going to be homeowners!

But not so fast. As the process unfolded, some issues kept popping up. We started the first mortgage process in November 2015. An issue would pop up making us have to re-start the process. Then mid-process again the second time around, another issue popped up. Finally, it took a 3rd time around. Each time required an appraisal. We even had the same appraiser and when he came out, he was like, "Wow, 3 times already for this transaction". We were like yeah, this is crazy. We started to have doubts that this transaction was going to go through. We had done so much work to the house before we even moved in. If this doesn't go through, we are going to have to find a place to live because my brothers were patiently waiting for their shares of the buyout.

I started feeling down and discouraged but then, it started going smoothly. So, after these delays, we finally get to closing. And when is closing? March of 2016 thus 3/16! There it is again. I was like wow, now this is really starting to get crazy. Can this really be just another 3:16 coincidence? Here it is, my mother's home, the one large asset she had to pass on to her children. The closing gets delayed twice which pushed it to March of 2016. Maybe to some people this would still just be coincidence, but after starting to see the 3:16 signs multiple times in my life at precise moments, it's starting to be a trend. Maybe it's my mom's way of still telling us everything is going to be ok and just trust in the Gospel.

I share this 3:16 sign with my wife again and now she herself is starting to think that it is more than coincidence. She started to wonder to herself about these 3:16's I've been seeing.

CHAPTER 5
My Best Friend

The crew as I call them, were my special group of friends that I worked with during my first stint with Cumberland Farms right after high school. The crew grew a little bigger by each of us introducing our friends that we already knew to the existing crew. This was the crew that I already mentioned a little bit about before who helped drag me out of my shyness around girls. They introduced me to the night club scene and the online dating and chat rooms. Every week we would go out to the club. These were the fun and crazy times in my life. I could probably write a whole book on those 2-3 years of fun and crazy times in my very early 20's.

I still keep in touch with everyone from that group. It's a

lot different now. A lot of us now have families and/or career responsibilities, so we don't see each other nearly as much as back in the day. But we make it important to stay in touch. I love all those guys. They will always be the crew.

Now just like any group of friends, you are naturally closer to certain ones more than others just by the nature of your interests, etc. That was no different with this group of friends. We were all close, but there were a couple that I was closer to more than others. One in particular was my friend Rafal. As time went on, he just became someone I totally trusted. I always felt like I could confide in him, and he wouldn't be judgmental or anything like that. I could confide in him my true feelings about certain things going on in my life and I felt comfortable.

We would talk about all kinds of things from girls to sports to career stuff to possibly moving to Florida. Sometimes we joked with each other that we were like a couple of "chicks" (as our young 20-year-old versions of ourselves would refer to girls as back then), due to our longer conversations on the phone. I would hang up and be like, damn I kind of feel like a "chick", we just talked for like a half hour, ha-ha. But anyway, we just clicked. We understood each other. We got each other. He was like a brother to me. In some ways I would confide more in him than my own brothers, even though both of whom I was extremely close with. But with family sometimes you just worry about the judgmental piece or what they are going to think. Sometimes you have to keep friend conversations separate from family.

My first Florida trip with the guys was just unbelievable. The warm weather, the night club scene, the beaches, the theme parks. I was just in awe of everything down there. I was hooked and started planning out annual trips. My friend Rafal also loved Florida. We would talk about Florida all the time and contemplated moving there.

Soon after, we both were promoted to management roles at our companies – him at Cumberland Farms, me at Walmart, and we were seriously planning on moving down and transferring down there. We went down there on a guy's trip and hit up the clubs and were definitely feeling a move was a real possibility.

That same trip, there were two phone calls that changed my thinking on my plans. The first was from my mother who told me that she had been diagnosed with breast cancer. This was her first cancer, not the one that she ended up passing away from. She told me she didn't want me to worry while I was on vacation and contemplated not telling me until I got back so I would enjoy my vacation, but she wanted me to know at the same time as everyone else. I teared up on the phone and it got very emotional. This was my mom. I was devastated. When you hear that word cancer you think the worst.

I immediately called my eventual wife. We were still in the friends/ not sure what we are mode. I told her about my mom and what was going on. She was very comforting as she always was. I told her how I was thinking of moving to Florida but now was not sure. She then told me for the first time that she loved me.

I didn't know how to respond at first. I knew I loved her too but hadn't heard her say it to me before. Soon after I got back home is when we decided to move in together and the rest is history as they say.

So back to Rafal, one memorable moment on this trip prior to these phone calls, is that we were sitting there on Daytona Beach and some girl comes up to us. Here we are, two single guys sitting on the beach and some random girl approaches both of us. We were both like – oh cool this girl is coming to talk to us. But it was nothing like we suspected. She starts talking about the Bible and God.

That was a subject me and Rafal never talked about. I had no idea what his thoughts were about it. We were like the party together guy friends. Not the church going together friends. I told her that I believed in Jesus and the Bible verse John 3:16. This was a couple years after I went through all of those negative emotions and had that first 3:16 t-shirt moment that may have saved my life. It was still a very private moment for me and did not bring it up to either of them, I just simply told her that I did believe.

My attention was immediately drawn to Rafal when it was his turn to speak. I was very curious what he believed. He told her that he did believe in God. And the three of us talked about Jesus for a little while and then the girl went on her way, probably to go talk to others on the beach about it. It was just a memorable moment that always stuck with me.

I considered Rafal my best friend. We always stayed in

touch very regularly for many years. Even once we were both in relationships and each eventually got married. We would still make time to hang out, watch a Patriots game together. We loved to go tailgating to the games, sometimes we would have a big crew there, sometimes it was just us and frying up a turkey for the first time. Of all of my friends, he was the one that I would hang out with more where it was just us vs with the whole crew. With us, it was just a lot of laughs, very similar sense of humor. He got me into the Dave Chappelle Lil Jon skits when they first were coming out. Yeeeaah! Whaaat? and Okaaay! were part of our normal vocabulary.

Unfortunately, tragedy struck in his life as well. It was during a time where we were not as close as we had been. This was many years after that Florida trip. Just to paint the picture for you, this was after my father-in-law, after my mother passed away, after buying the family home. It was just a busy time with work and everything else. He had some things going on in his life with changing careers and was busy with that so we just didn't talk as much or connect much.

I received a text message one morning from a good friend, who was also a member of the crew – "Raf passed away yesterday". I was stunned. I couldn't believe what I was reading. It didn't seem real to me. Although I hadn't seen him as often as I used to, I still considered him my best friend. I was devastated and even more so knowing that I hadn't seen him recently.

I'm not sure the exact cause of death if it was heart attack or what, but he definitely had some health issues at the end that I was not even aware of, which made me even more distraught. His family is very private, and I didn't want to even bring it up and ask more questions. It has been tough to get complete closure without knowing all the details, but I respect the family and their privacy. I just don't feel right asking a bunch of questions. I could tell they were all crushed by this. The service was extremely sad. No one could believe that Raf was gone. He was way too young to be gone -not even 40 years old.

Just the thought I would never be able to have another conversation with him. He was the one I trusted so much with my thoughts and feelings about different things. To not have that person to call or talk to ever again really hurt.

So, the day I receive the devastating text message, I call my friend and we talk about it. I'm in a depressed funk. I go to Walmart to do some shopping for the house. I'm going through 4 gallons of milk per week, which I will explain a little more on why later on in this book. That's when I received yet another sign. I grabbed the whole milk out of the cooler on this same day I found out about Rafal and what is the expiration date on the milk? It is 3/16. I'm just blown away again. I'm like wow, these 3:16 signs are starting to get out of hand. Here I am depressed as all hell that I am never going to be able to talk to him again and I see this 3:16.

My mood immediately gets picked up. I feel oddly upbeat and encouraged. I truly felt like it was from him saying, don't worry about me, I'm good. You can still talk to me in your thoughts and prayers. And I have done that on multiple occasions. I almost feel like he's a guardian angel up there helping to look after me sometimes. And I also look back at that day on the beach all those years ago in Daytona where he said that he did believe. So maybe that was no coincidence either.

It's not that I just see 3:16 signs, it is the timing of them. It's seeing them on the exact days or at the exact times that certain things happen. These signs were really starting to accumulate and now I decided I'm going to document this. It's becoming quite a bit here. I'm looking at the milk on the floor in my truck and I tell myself "I have to get a picture of this". Not that I ever planned to write this book, I just wanted to have some proof for myself in case I ever decided to tell anyone these stories or just remind myself of what I've seen. My wife was definitely starting to be, if not already, on board with these 3:16's. As every time I showed her these things, she was in awe just like me. Another photo I took, and I know it's a stretch now, but the receipt from our lunch we had also on this same day as the milk, was $16.03. I know it's not 3:16 exactly but it grabbed my attention enough for me to take a photo of it as well.

Figure 5-1: The expiration date on the milk of 3/16/20

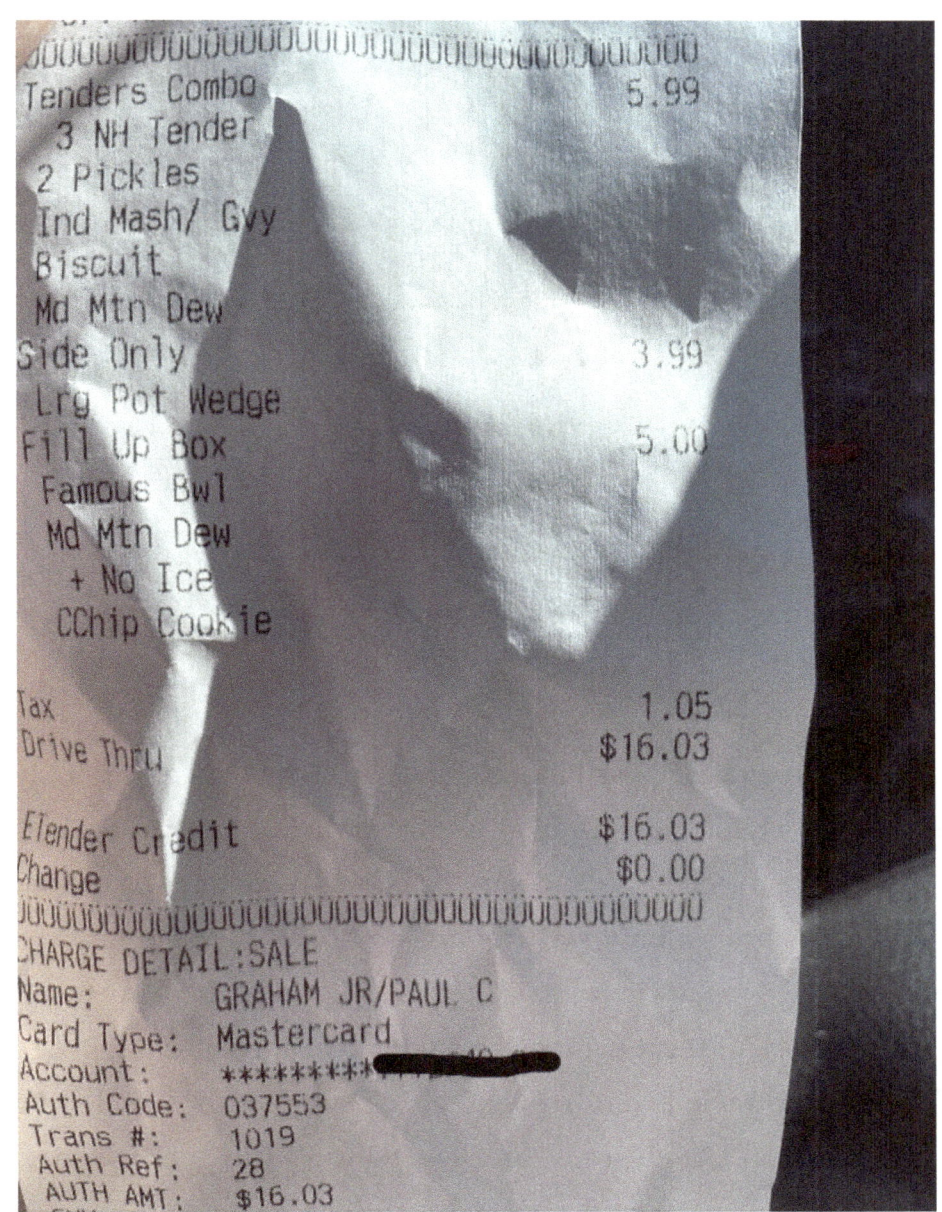

Figure 5-2: Yes, it's a stretch. Lunch was $16.03 that same day

CHAPTER 6
My Uncle

My uncle Bob is kind of the key to the whole puzzle. My father's passing away is what started the chain of events that led me to believe in 3:16. But the puzzle piece that was placed just at the proper time was my uncle Bob. My father's death is what started my uncle on that journey to find out where my father was now and if there was any chance to see him again.

By that tragic event happening, it catapulted my uncle into learning about God, Jesus, and the John 3:16 Gospel message. A lot of souls were perhaps saved by this one event. My uncle would spread the word as much as he could when the right opportunities presented themselves. He didn't just go around preaching to everyone, that would just turn people away. But if he saw an opening to bring it up, he would go for it. He would tell me stories of when auto part delivery drivers would deliver at his body shop and once in a while, the conversation would start up. Whether he saw a tattoo of a lost loved one or somehow the subject would get started. My uncle would share his story of how his brother had passed, the tragedy of how it happened, and how he sought answers. He would tell me that what stood out to him any time that he witnessed to someone is that they were so focused and listened with intent to his every word. He would say that was the power of the holy spirit working.

He would tell me stories of Jehovah's Witnesses coming to his door. Most people don't answer the door or if they do, they grab the paperwork quickly and try to get that door shut as fast as possible. But my uncle enjoyed it when they came. He would turn the tables and start asking them questions. He would tell them that they had it all backwards. Now I don't know about Jehovah's Witnesses, I never studied them or exactly what they believe. But my uncle was convinced that they had it all wrong.

My uncle was not always this way. He was not a real religious man in his early days. It was great to see what he turned into. This man became someone who thirsted for the knowledge of God. He studied, read the Bible, really got involved in the church. He would play on the basketball team, the softball team, and joined the men's ministry groups. Over time, he amassed quite a bit of knowledge about the Christian faith. He even got to the point where he would start critiquing the Pastor. His most recent

Pastor told me that Bob would be waiting for him after service and would critique his message. It was done in a good way and the pastor was always ready to face Bob at the end of service.

If my father didn't pass away at that time, who knows if my uncle would have ever turned into this version of himself. Who knows if I would have ever made it to that church and ever heard the Gospel and that worship song in just the right way so that I would believe in it.

It's funny how close he was to never even making it in the door to Grace Gospel Church. He told me that someone he knew kept asking him to go to his church – Grace Gospel Church. My uncle was used to traditional churches from any times that he did go. Even though he was searching for answers, he wasn't seeking out Grace Gospel Church, in some ways it sought out him. This member of the church kept asking him to attend, he would tell my uncle that this church was "Alive" and growing. He said that the Catholic Church Bob belonged to was a "Dead" church. It was stagnant and not growing.

My uncle skeptically went there one day, probably wanting to point out everything wrong with the church. But quite the opposite happened. The church totally changed his life.

Although, as the years went by, Bob ended up switching churches. But he would still always reminisce about the glory days of Grace Gospel Church and how great of a church it was during that era and how important it was in his life.

The ironic part during the day of my uncle's funeral service is that during the ride from the funeral home to Bob's new church, we drove by Grace Gospel Church. It was only fitting that we would drive by the church that changed his life in such a tremendous way.

I can't thank my uncle enough for what he did for my life. If it wasn't for him, I really don't know where I would be in life. Besides my wife, he was the one I would also bring up some of these 3:16 signs that I had seen to. Actually, I would tell him and his wife as they were so close in their relationship. You rarely saw one without the other one. He believed in them with me. He thought it was cool that I was seeing these signs. He then told me some crazy more than coincidence type stories that had happened to him in his life. It just further fueled my belief that these signs are really real.

Unfortunately, my uncle passed away of Covid-19. He was relatively young in his early 60's. He was active, he was in good shape. As scary as Covid was with everything going on, everyone I saw in my personal life that had it, including myself, contracted it, got sick, but then recovered. I'm still in shock that my uncle never did recover. He went from good health to death relatively quickly. My uncle passed away on April 22. This was oddly also my wife's birthday. I feel like there is meaning behind that aspect of it, but I haven't totally figured it out.

Now the sign that came from this whole ordeal was not exactly 3:16. But it still really blew my mind as it unfolded. The best way to describe it to you is to share with you the eulogy that

I read at his funeral service. I apologize if it is not exactly correct grammar or structured properly. These are just my notes I used as a guide. I didn't want to change anything. Here are the exact notes for my speech:

"So the last few days all I'm thinking about is Uncle Bob. I'm looking at pictures and watching all these videos and seeing what memories I have of Bob . And I realize how many things Bob was at. He spent his TIME on me. He cared about me, he LOVED me. And it made me start to tear up. He was there for me. He supported me by attending all kinds of stuff. He ran our whole renewal of vows service. He read at my wedding. I can't think of a Graham Bash he and Debbie didn't go to. And many years, stayed late and until the end. Just last year dancing the night away prob midnight I don't know. Was he always feeling up to it? No prob not. Was there times he could have easily said - Something came up I can't go. But he didn't. He came and supported me and my plans. He spent his time on me. He wasn't just a good uncle. He was a great uncle.

I watched my wedding DVD. There he is a reader. Dressed all nice. There he is right there at the end still dancing with all my 20 year old friends. There he is spending his TIME with me.

I started thinking of a message that Pastor Martel at Grace Gospel Church gave when I first started attending. He talked about TIME being the greatest gift you can give someone. That once it's spent YOU CAN NEVER GET IT BACK, ITS Gone. ITS THE MOST PRECIOUS GIFT YOU CAN GIVE TO SOMEONE.

That message hit my heart and I still think of it till this day.

So back then Grace Gospel had this tape ministry with the weekly messages on them. And Bob loved those tapes. I remember him taking me, just me and him to go play pickup basketball games at Taunton High gym at night. And he would listen to these tapes on the way up. And he gave me some.

Well I remember he gave me the one about TIME. So anyway, I'm preparing to talk to you all today and I'm thinking I'm gonna go look for this tape so I can listen to the message again and see if anything pops out to me. So I start looking though my old tapes. I check the basement. Not there. I check everywhere in the house. Not there. I'm looking everywhere so Now I'm on a mission to find this tape. So I remember I have some old camcorder tapes in my storage container. I check there and bam I find a tape from Grace Gospel Church. The only Grace Gospel Tape I have left. The message label on it is "No More Tears". Kind of pertains to what's going on right now. Just out of curiosity, I'm like when was this message, how old is it? The tapes had the dates on them. So I look at the date and I just shake my head and laugh and look up and say "That's you Bob, that's def you" The date is April 22,1997 - April 22 just a few days ago is the date Bob passed on to be with God.

Call it coincidence if you want, but I immediately took it as a message from Bob. A message that he's telling me he's up there and he's looking down on me and wanted to give me that sign.

So I'm on this journey now that brought me to this one and only tape left from Grace Gospel church. So I listen to the tape and it kinda blew my mind even more.

It wasn't the tape about the importance of Time but it was 100% about what is going on right now. It was a memorial service message. It talked about Heaven and what it's like, what's in the Bible about it. A whole message applying to what is going on right now. I wanted to hear what it was Bob wanted me to hear and share. And this is what I came up with:

Pastor talked about the person who passed and asked these questions that I apply to Bob-

If there was one thing that you could do that could be a blessing to him, wouldn't you want to do it? If he had one last dying request that he would wake up out of the coma and ask of you, wouldn't you want to honor it?

And knowing Bob and what was important to him, I think I know what his request would probably be. He would want you to seek GOD. To learn about him, to research him and be sure that when you die, you will be in heaven - with Bob. Your day is coming where you will be facing what Bob faced. So I pray that you face it in peace and confidence of where you're going.

After these signs from Bob with the tape - esp the date on it- I rest a little easier now. I truly believe that everything he believed in with the Gospel and John 3:16 is all true. He's up there now and he wanted me to know and to tell you all. There's no bigger truth to know in this world than that of the Gospel. And if you don't know what it is, you should look into it.

As Pastor also said - If I'm wrong about heaven and hell and you're right, what happens? I really have nothing to lose. We all end up in the ground anyway big deal.

But if I'm right and you're wrong, you have everything to lose. Think about that for a minute. What if you're wrong? So I would say - at-least do your research and try to find out for yourself the truth. Don't go by what you always believed or what your parents believed or even what I'm telling you I believe. Go find out for yourself. Challenge yourself and go where the journey takes you. Have an open mind and open heart. It's the most important journey Bob would want you to go on before your last day comes.

Thank you everyone. "

Figure 6-1: Cassette Tape was from 4/22/97

In Memory of

Robert A. Graham

~ *April 22, 2021*

The memory of a good person is a blessing.
Proverbs 10:7

Figure 6-2: My Uncle Bob passed away 4/22/21

BONUS CHAPTER
My Uncle's Celebration

S o, I added this chapter into my uncle's story. This actually occurred while I was just about finished writing this book and just adding the finishing touches. It was so much that I had to include it. And 3:16 definitely plays a role in this story.

My uncle Bob's wife and daughter planned a celebration of life get together for my Uncle Bob, two years after his passing. April 22, the anniversary of his death date, happened to fall on a Saturday, so they planned to have it on this exact anniversary date. As previously mentioned, that date actually coincidentally is also my wife's birthday.

My wife, the big breakfast lover that she is, chose IHOP for her celebration location. She invited her immediate family – mother, sister and her husband, niece, etc. The plan was to go celebrate her birthday in the afternoon and then to go celebrate my uncle's life at my aunt's house in the evening. A few days before the life celebration party, my aunt unfortunately had to cancel as she had just gotten sick and was just not up to hosting a get together plus the weather was not looking great for this outside planned event. She decided it was best to re-schedule it.

So, April 22nd comes along, we get into the car to go to IHOP. After I start the car, I happen to look at the vehicle miles and I'm like "Oh that's pretty cool, look honey – 316". The miles on the odometer were 13169. So, I snapped a photo before I backed out of the driveway. It was a cool moment being on April 22nd, but nothing crazy. We went about our day to IHOP.

My wife had a great birthday celebration. My wife continues to say how wonderful it was that her family was there to celebrate with her. So, after spending over a couple of hours there of good times and laughs, we headed out to the car. I checked Facebook and saw that my cousin had posted a picture of herself with her mother and father. She wrote something about missing her father on this day. My heart just goes out to them when I read this post. It was such a contrast in emotions between celebrating with my wife and also knowing that this is the same anniversary date that we lost my uncle Bob. I know how close the three of them were as a family and how devasting it must be for them to have to go through this.

I start reminiscing about the old times with them, having

grown up 2 houses down. I start commenting on the post with my feelings and giving my support to them on this difficult anniversary date. As I am in the middle of typing, a very similar situation to the one that occurred with my father-in-law almost re-occurs.

There was this one song that my aunt played for my uncle while he was in the hospital towards the end. It was "An Easter Hallelujah" by Cassandra and Callahan. The remnants of hospital Covid-19 protocols were still in effect when my uncle was sick in the hospital, so not everyone was able to visit him. The visiting procedures were very strict. My aunt said that when she played this song for him and sent it to him, he would get very emotional during the song. She told us this story at the memorial service after she had them play this song in his honor because he loved it so much. It's a very touching song to listen to.

So back to the car at IHOP. I'm responding to the Facebook post about my uncle and as I'm typing, this song comes on in the car. Now, it's not as much of a crazy coincidence as with my father-in-law when I heard that Enya song come on, because that was on the actual radio. This time, my uncle's song was from my wife's playlist of ITUNES songs. So, the odds are not as extremely stacked against this happening by coincidence, but still with the hundreds of songs that she has, for this one song to randomly shuffle in on this date at this time of typing, did make me immediately look at my wife and say "Wow. That's crazy that this song just came on while I'm typing this and thinking about him."

But now is when it really starts to get to be like - Wow are you kidding me right now? All of these things I'm about to tell you about all happen in probably about a 10-minute span. I hear the song in the car as I'm typing. When I'm done typing, we drive out of the parking lot and head home. As we're driving, you can't help but notice this big sign where BJ's Warehouse is located. What's the gas price at BJ's? You will probably guess it by this point - $3.16! Again, It's not $3.17 or $3.15, its $3.16! Of course, my great wife, fully on board with me now noticing these things, quickly takes a picture.

So, I'm thinking about my aunt and my cousin and after reading the Facebook post, something is just tugging on my heart to go by and give them all hugs, just thinking about what they are going through on this anniversary date. But then I remember she is sick and it's probably not a great idea to go into the house and catch something that I can pass on to other people. I also think she probably just wants to rest and doesn't want company coming over.

I decided to call my aunt. I don't call my aunt much at all, most communication these days is done via text message. But in this case, I just wanted to have a conversation with her and hoped she was up to it. I call her up through the Bluetooth in the car so my wife can participate in the conversation also. So we call and thankfully she answers. It was great to hear her voice. We ask her how she's feeling, etc. I tell her I'm thinking about her and her family. She's wishing my wife a happy birthday. We're just having a nice conversation.

Then I see this truck pull directly in front of us. The license plate says "DRBOBS". I couldn't believe it. I'm like, my aunt is sick right now and here is a "DRBOBS" license plate on this anniversary day that the party was supposed to be. I actually interrupt her in mid-sentence and say "You won't believe what license plate just pulled in front of me! Dr. Bob's!" I joked and said, "Dr. Bob is coming to heal you!". She laughed and said, "I hope so!". I'm telling my wife "You got to get a picture of that and send it to her!" It was just a fun little moment.

I then proceeded to tell her about the other stuff that happened – hearing the Hallelujah song as I was responding to the Facebook post and then the gas price was $3.16 at BJ's that we just drove by. At which point, my wife pointed out was really weird because it was $2.99 not long ago, she said that was a big jump in that short amount of time. And I again I point out "And yeah to $3.16 of all numbers it could be today". My aunt was one of the select few that had heard any of these 3:16 stories as she was there with Bob sometimes when I confided in him and shared some of these very cool coincidences with him.

My aunt says "Wow, you see these things a lot". I laughed and said "Yeah". So, we ended the nice conversation and are close to home now. We get to the light at the intersection and have to stop. I look up and see the "DRBOBS" license plate is directly in front of us, and we are stopped so I tell my wife – "Oh look, its right there now. Now you can get a great picture of it". As she is taking it, this is when I was really like wowed, having a this is just getting crazy, jaw dropping kind of moment. I just happened to look at the car next to the truck we are behind and the license plate on that car is 316! I'm like this is crazy. I tell my wife "Honey, look at that car right there." She doesn't see anything standing out. I said, "No look at the license plate". She's like "Wow, 316"! So, she takes a quick picture of the two vehicles side by side. Remember this is after all of the other incidents in this book, so I'm in picture mode now when it comes to this stuff.

That was just the final piece that made me in awe of the moment. All of these occurring in a 10 minute or so span – The song in the car as I'm typing, driving by BJ's, and seeing the $3:16 gas price, the conversation with my aunt and seeing "DRBOBS" drive by, then getting to the streetlight and seeing "DRBOBS" on side of "316". Then I remembered back to the start of the day and seeing the odometer with 316 on it. I almost feel like it's Bob or someone just toying around with us up there sometimes. Maybe it's no coincidence that this array of little signs occurred on a very significant date related to the most religious, God seeking man that I knew who changed the course of my Christian believing life forever.

*Figure 6-3: The miles on our vehicle when we first started it
on the morning of 4/22/23*

Figure 6-4: The gas price at BJ's on 4/22/23

Figure 6-5: DRBOBS and 316 side by side on 4/22/23

CHAPTER 7
Real Estate

My journey into real estate did not go exactly the way I had planned it. In fact, there was no exact plan to go into real estate. It was the accumulation of little moments that happened. Let me explain.

So, if you remember back to the house chapter, I spoke about my working life journey. At that point I worked for a jail as a correction officer and was planning to work there for 20 years to set up my retirement. Well fast forward 7 ½ years and as everyone has probably learned in life, things change. Trying to predict a 20-year period is not always going to go the way you expect.

I'm just going to set the scene for you. I graduated from the academy, things are good. The first couple years are tough like all of the veteran officers tell you. You are trying to gain the respect of the senior officers along with the incarcerated individuals - inmates. You are trying to show that you can handle the job at a high level and respond to various situations that can arise in an instant. You can go from sitting quietly at a desk to seconds later responding to an incident filled with blood from inmates fighting or someone inflicting self-harm or you yourself performing CPR. Your adrenaline and emotions can really go from zero to 100 real fast.

I'm not going to dive into every aspect of the job or all of the things that just I've seen, and I was only there 7 ½ years, but as you can probably imagine there are some crazy events that occur.

But with all that said, I actually on some level didn't mind the job. I had the mindset to do my 20 years and get out of dodge. I met a lot of great officers and staff and built friendships that I still maintain today. I have a lot of respect for the officers and what they do there. The situations they don't hesitate to put themselves in and how they handle violent situations are just somethings to be commended. I was proud to be part of that team and work alongside my brothers and sisters there.

I enjoyed my job the most there when I was working in Booking and Intake. Every day, the facility would receive new inmates into custody who had to be booked in. Then we would also book inmates out who were being bailed out or released from custody. There was a lot of documentation needed for each inmate. We would have to learn how to read all of the court paperwork and input the information into the computer system, take fingerprints, photographs, etc,. You also had to be security minded and keep everyone safe by ensuring security procedures were met. This involved not having too many inmates out at the same time, keeping inmates secured in the cells until it was their turn to be booked in. It was about keeping everything working in an orderly, organized manner.

The incarcerated individuals did not always cooperate. You were working with individuals who did not want to be there, who were recently arrested for allegedly committed crimes, some of whom were under the influence of drugs or alcohol where the individual was detoxing. There was a large medical and mental health aspect to this area of the jail as well.

Not all areas of the jail were like this. There are so many posts throughout the jail. Some posts were more difficult than this post, some were easier. I liked this area because it felt more like my previous jobs. It required a high sense of urgency, where you had to keep up with the daily flow of inmates coming in and out of the facility. It required completing multiple tasks that came along with this process in a relatively fast paced manner. Also, I want to notate that not all incarcerated individuals were disrespectful or acted violently. There were a number of individuals who were extremely cooperative and respectful. But of course, there were a number of whom that were quite the opposite of that.

When the conditions at the jail changed and when my personal situation changed, were both actually around the same timeframe. During the height of Covid and the months that followed, we saw a dramatic decrease in staffing levels. Officers were leaving for other careers, some just leaving altogether. It was almost like a mass exodus. Now there always was turnover in the facility as many correction officers used this position as a steppingstone to court officer, police officer, or other law enforcement career options.

But this time frame was different. Officers were going back to their previous employers, some to completely different fields, some with no jobs lined up. Just to give you an idea of how it works there is that there are a lot of posts that need to be staffed at all times. There are 3 shifts, like most 24-hour operations - 1st 2nd, and 3rd shift. If there are not enough officers available to fill all of the necessary posts for the next shift, officers from the previous shift would be forced to stay for a double shift. There was a system to fill open necessary posts where the posts were first offered as voluntary overtime, but most open necessary posts were typically filled with "forced" mandatory overtime.

In these scenarios, most likely you would be staying for a double shift. So, for example if you worked 3pm-11pm and then were mandatory forced, instead of leaving at 11pm, you would most likely be staying overnight until 7am. And if you were scheduled for that next day, would still have to be back in time for your 3pm shift. Keep in mind this is a jail setting so it's not like just walking into the building and your relief is free to go. There is a whole security process to entering the building, getting your assignment and any notes of the day, then making your way to your post. Once on post then the previous shift officer is free to exit, once again going through security protocol. So, shifts are slightly longer than 8 hours and when you are forced for a 16-hour shift, you don't always get a full 8 hours in between shifts.

Now some officers like the extra income and extra shifts and some do not. For the beginning of my career, I did not want extra money or extra shifts. I worked so many long hours in retail that I really enjoyed the 40-hour work weeks. I came in at a time where there was not a lot of forced overtime. Plus, it helped that I graduated close to the top of my academy, so I had higher seniority than most of my classmates. So, I never experienced a great deal of forced overtime, of course there was some, but not regularly. The way the mandatory overtime worked was that officers with less seniority would be forced first.

Then circumstances in my life changed where I did want the extra income. I began to voluntarily stay for overtime on multiple shifts per week. During the covid year when the staffing levels extremely decreased, it didn't affect me too much because I was already committed to taking voluntary overtime.

Conditions just continued to worsen. Staffing levels started to get even lower and in a bad place. Sometimes there were not enough officers on one shift to even stay and cover all of the necessary open posts on the next shift because so many were already there for back to back shifts. So, a tremendous number of officers were getting forced overtime whether they wanted to stay or not. Officers with 20 years of seniority who wouldn't even think it was a possibility to get forced in years prior, were now getting forced regularly.

Getting forced is not just about working extra hours, it just takes a toll on people's personal lives. They have responsibilities outside of work. Maybe they are supposed to pick up their child from daycare, or have appointments, schedules, want to exercise at the gym, or just want to see their family at some point during the day. Then not to mention, the medical health risks involved with this little to no sleep work schedule especially trying to figure out when to also fit in your daily life tasks.

This is a job that you need to be mentally alert for to perform it at the proper level. A lot of people are drinking energy drinks and doing whatever they can to remain awake and alert daily. Yes, some posts are quite busy for the majority of the shift and a lot of crazy events do occur. But there are also some posts that are called "eyeball watches" where you literally have to sit in a chair for an 8-hour shift and watch someone sleep the majority of that time because you need to ensure they do not hurt themselves. Try staying awake on that post after getting little to no sleep. Sugar and caffeine become a vital part of your diet. I would compare it to sitting on your couch at home by yourself (although not a comfortable couch, instead a very lightly padded chair) and watching a blank TV screen for 8 hours.

So, a lot of officers understandably decided this was not for them anymore. But unfortunately, what does that cause? More open necessary posts and forced overtime. It was like a vicious cycle. It did not help that the hiring process is long and selective. It makes total sense to have it set up that way. You want background checks, fingerprints, interviews, drug screening, etc. before you allow someone security access throughout a jail facility. They only have one or two training academies per year. That also makes sense to me due to the number of resources that it takes to train new recruits in the academy. It makes sense to train them in groups. But the facility could not keep up with replacing the officers who left. Plus, recruiting was becoming increasingly difficult because previously, most applicants were referrals from officers and staff. With forced mandatory overtime at the level that it was, no officer was recruiting anyone they knew to work there.

Even though I volunteered for overtime, I was also forced to do mandatory overtime. Eventually this took a toll on my health. I'm not going to get into all of my medical issues that were going on, but it scared me. I knew I needed a change. Even if I wanted to stop taking overtime shifts, I would still be forced to take them.

I knew I was at a crossroad, and it was difficult. I needed a high-level income. But I could not continue in this work environment the way it was going. Healthwise, I really felt like I would not be around a whole lot longer going the way I was going. But then I would mentally go back to the idea that this career was my retirement plan. I didn't t have another retirement plan. It was so engrained in my head that this was the game plan for the next

12-13 years or so until I hit the required milestone for retirement and be able to collect the pension they offered, that I didn't think of any other options.

But If I didn't improve my health, it wouldn't have mattered if I only had 1 year left until retirement. Being alive and healthy with no career is better than the alternative.

So, I made an appointment with my doctor to be evaluated and discuss all the issues that were concerning me. But this was a big decision, I was not ready to throw away all of my time I put in towards a retirement pension.

Before the appointment, I wanted to research all of my options. I looked up the Leave of Absence Policy to see what that was all about. That was the first 3:16 sign that eventually led me to real estate, but not before a lot of other things happened first. At this point in my life, I've experienced quite a few 3:16 moments in my life so now I'm much more aware of them and probably sensitive to noticing them. The flood gates were about to open soon with these as I will get into.

When I looked into the policies regarding a Leave of Absence, this is the title of the section that it was: 03.01.16 Family and Medical Leave (FMLA). It stood out to me right away that maybe this is the right path. But I was going to speak with my doctor and figure everything out. I printed out the document so I could read the whole thing over.

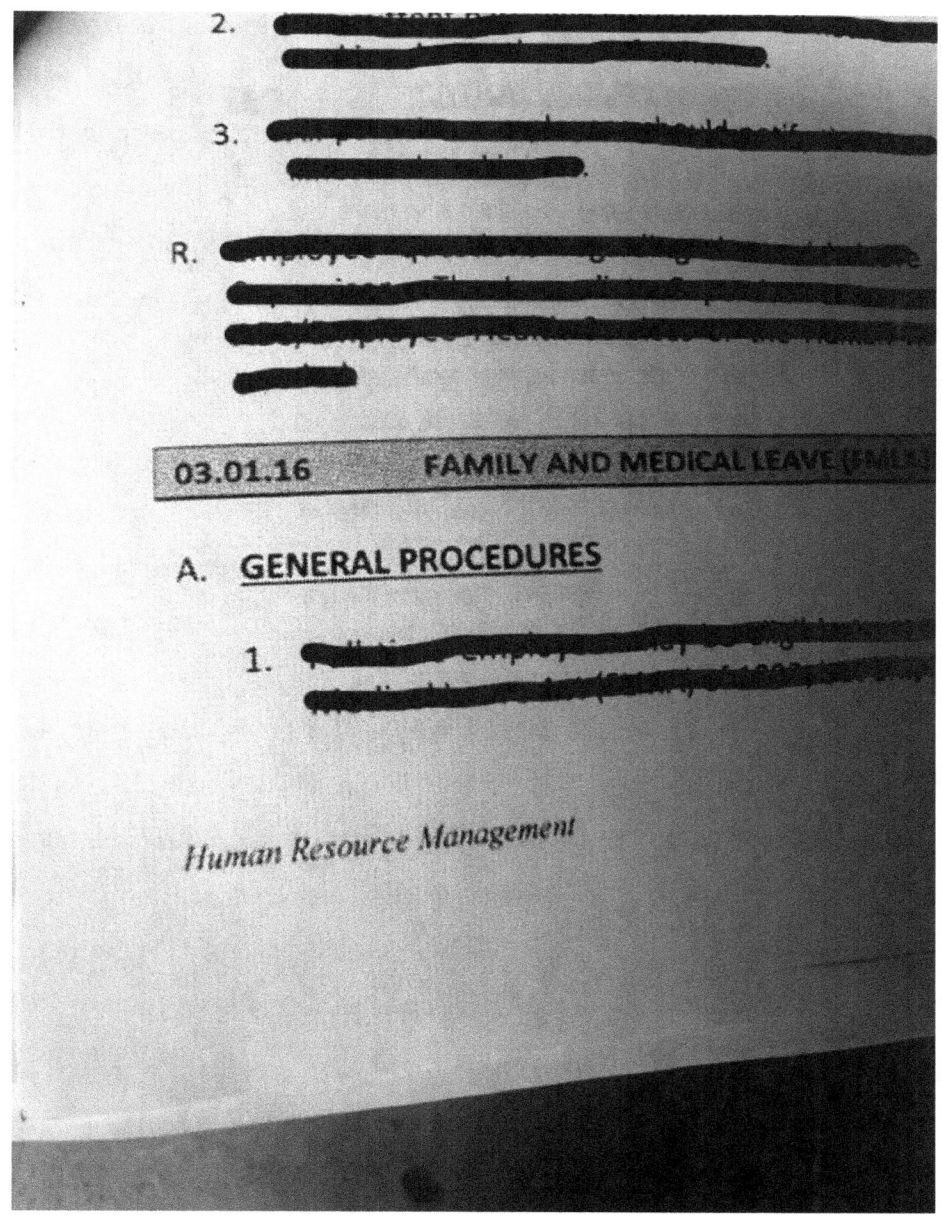

Figure 7-1 – FMLA Section Number 03.01.16. Not exact 3:16, but close enough to notice

After meeting with my medical providers, it was determined that the best course of action was to go on the (FMLA) Leave of Absence while steps were taken to correct the medical issues that I had going on. After monitoring and evaluating the results of those steps, it would also allow some time to consider if returning to the correction officer role was going to be the right move for me going forward.

Ultimately, I ended up deciding not to continue in my role as correction officer. It was difficult to throw away the time I had invested there, but after speaking with medical professionals throughout the whole process, this was what seemed to be the best decision. I also did a lot of soul searching and contemplating what was best for my personal life.

What else should I pursue? I was not entirely sure. I started thinking about things that I liked and what else I would like to do with my life. One option I had was that I really loved our timeshare properties in Florida. My wife and I had purchased them before we were even engaged. We used them every year and loved them. We really loved Florida and had considered moving there but ultimately had not because we wanted to stay closer to our family and friends.

I started to think about all the possibilities and selling timeshares was always something that I thought about in the back of my mind. Every time that you stay at the timeshare, you have the opportunity to listen to updates and there is usually a sales pitch at the end if you are interested in purchasing additional points to get more use time with the timeshare. Being that person on the other side of that table always stuck out in my head as something that I was interested in doing.

It seemed like something I could do well because I truly believed in the timeshares, and we owned them ourselves. Even without any of their sales training, I could certainly tell someone what excited me about them. The memories I've shared while staying at them. We got to take my mother there, who never travelled anywhere really, let alone all the way to Florida. My wife got to bring her whole family including her now passed on father there. One time we went on a friend's trip and my best friend Rafal and his girlfriend at the time stayed with us. The memories we had there spending time with people who had now passed away were just priceless.

I inquired about what it entails to work there and spoke with some very helpful people. They tell me how much they love working for the company. They tell me how much they enjoy living in Florida. They tell me how much income I can expect to earn – which was far more than what I had earned my whole life even with overtime at the jail. They encourage me to do it. The main issue they tell me is that I would need a Florida real estate license. So, I'm excited, we were actually contemplating relocating to Florida, but one issue still remained. We still were not ready to leave our family and friends.

But it gets me thinking - If I'm going to go get my real estate license, why not do real estate where I live in Massachusetts?

Then we can still be close to our families? At the end of the day, we have to go where the income will be, but if we can stay here in the process, let me look into it.

So, I reached out to a real estate broker that I graduated high school with. She is extremely helpful, we meet, go over everything. She explains to me what to expect in this profession. She excites me with income potential. But most importantly, it aligns with my goals and my personality. If I work hard, I will see results. It is mainly a profession about helping people. The income will be there, just focus on helping people and be a resource for people. That is what I always wanted to be for people – a resource for help. There are not that many feel good careers as good as that one. Plus, I feel like that is my personality already.

Plus, real estate is something I can get behind. I believe in it being a great investment. It's a great feeling when you own your own home or start to build financial wealth through leveraging real estate.

Another positive was that you had control over your own schedule. Yeah, the hours would be long, but you would not miss your children's soccer games, football games, basketball games, etc. I was told of the negatives also, be prepared to have no income for 6 months to 1 year. There are a lot of realtor fees associated with the profession both monthly and annually. But after our conversation, I was pumped, I was excited. This is exactly what I was looking for.

I took the real estate licensing course, studied, and bam passed the test! It was so exciting! Many people said it was difficult to pass the first time and not to get discouraged, but I was fortunate, and I passed on the first try!

As I started to get into real estate, the 3:16's just kept coming at me. It was almost like little signs along the way to remind me that I was making the correct decision. Because taking on this career was a giant leap of faith. It is 100% commission and no guarantees of anything. I put my faith in God that I was taking the right plunge.

It started with the 03.01.16 Family and Medical Leave (FMLA) which made me feel that the LOA from the jail was the right line of thinking.

After I took my real estate course, we decided to take a spur of the moment road trip to Florida. We were going to keep it cheap. We still had our timeshare vacation planned for the end of the year. We drove down and stayed in a cheap hotel near the theme parks. I'm in the middle of doing laundry at the hotel. I have one load in the wash and of course it's the only washing machine available, so I have to wait to do the second load. I go back to the room until it's close to the time it will be done.

I go back to the laundry room so I can switch over the first load to the dryer and put the second load into the washing machine. My plan is to do these two loads quick so we can get to the theme park. I get there and there is an older lady there waiting by the washing machine for my first load to finish so she can put her load in. I mention that I was about to switch to my second load but for her to go ahead because she was there waiting. She asks me what my plans are for the day. I told her we are going to Universal Studios. She tells me "Well this is our last day, and we are just staying in", she then says, "I'll tell you what, why don't you go first but before you take your laundry out, can you just come knock on my room door to let me know so I can get the machine next?" I ask "Are you sure? You were waiting here first." She tells me "Yes, it's no problem at all. Just don't forget to come knock on my door. I don't want to you to get to the parks too late."

What an amazing gesture, I thought. I ask her "What's the room number?" "316" she says. My mouth must have dropped to the floor. In case she noticed my facial expression, I say, "I'm sorry, it's just a religious famous bible verse where I see that number a lot'" Have I ever met someone like this and had them tell me their room number before? No. Has anyone I ever ran into in any hotel ever, told me their room number before in my entire life? No, this is the only time this has happened. This was like a once in a lifetime event and it happened to be 316. Not a huge event by any stretch of the imagination, but enough for me to go back to the room and tell my wife about it and she thought it was just cool as me.

So, I've passed my real estate exam and I'm designing my logos for everything. This is where the signs really just start rolling in. I'm like ok c'mon man, is this really true? Are all of these signs really happening? I am just continuously being fed 316 signs that tell me I'm on the right path. By this point, I'm taking photos and screenshots whenever they pop up. And I'm not forcing any of these to happen, they are just happening and rolling.

So, in this logo in the photo. I already have the circle of fire ring as an image so I can't change the size of it, maybe It is possible but I'm brand new to this designing aspect of things, so I'm leaving the circle alone and I'm just adding the letters inside of it. I figure out the font style I want, I play with the effects of it. I'm trying to figure out how big to make the font. I get it right where it needs to be. What is the font size that fits exactly where I need it to be? 316 font size! I took an up-close picture of that as well.

Figure 7-2: PG Real Estate Logo Design Image showing perfect size font to fit inside the circle)

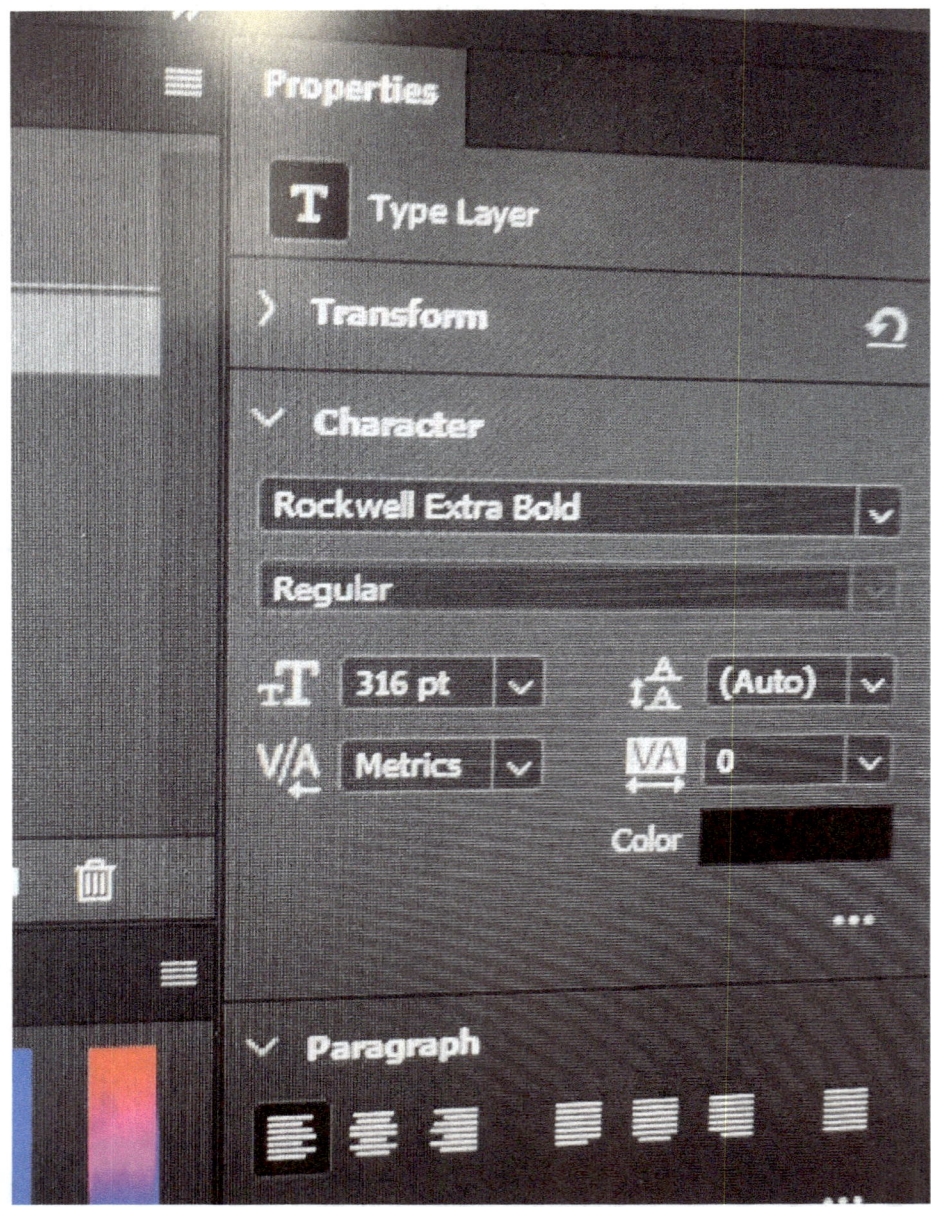

Figure 7-3: Up Close Image of the Font Size of PG Real Estate Logo Design Image showing perfect size font

I notice the following files as I'm editing videos for my YouTube channel:

Figure 7-4: This one here is 3:16:21

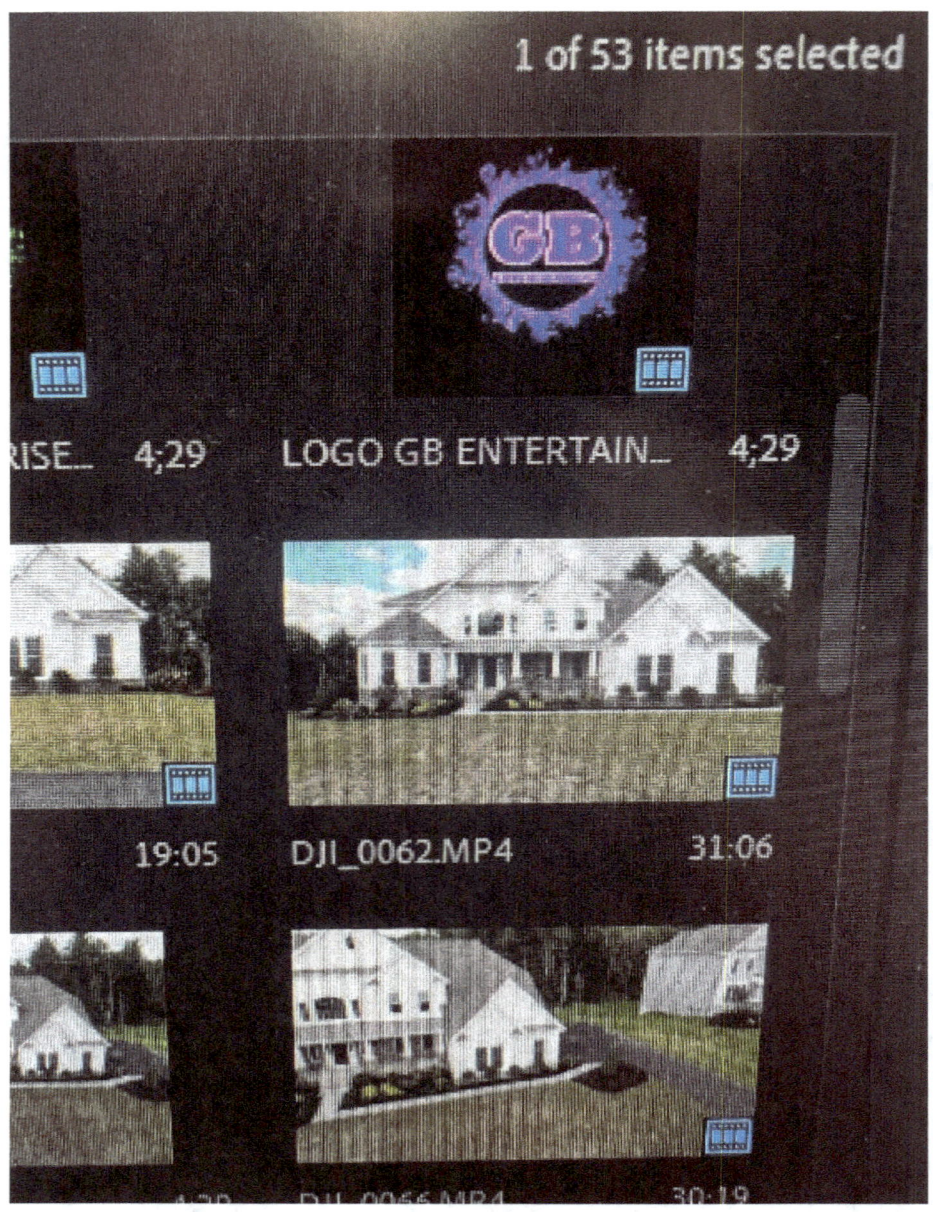

Figure 7-5: This one is 31:06

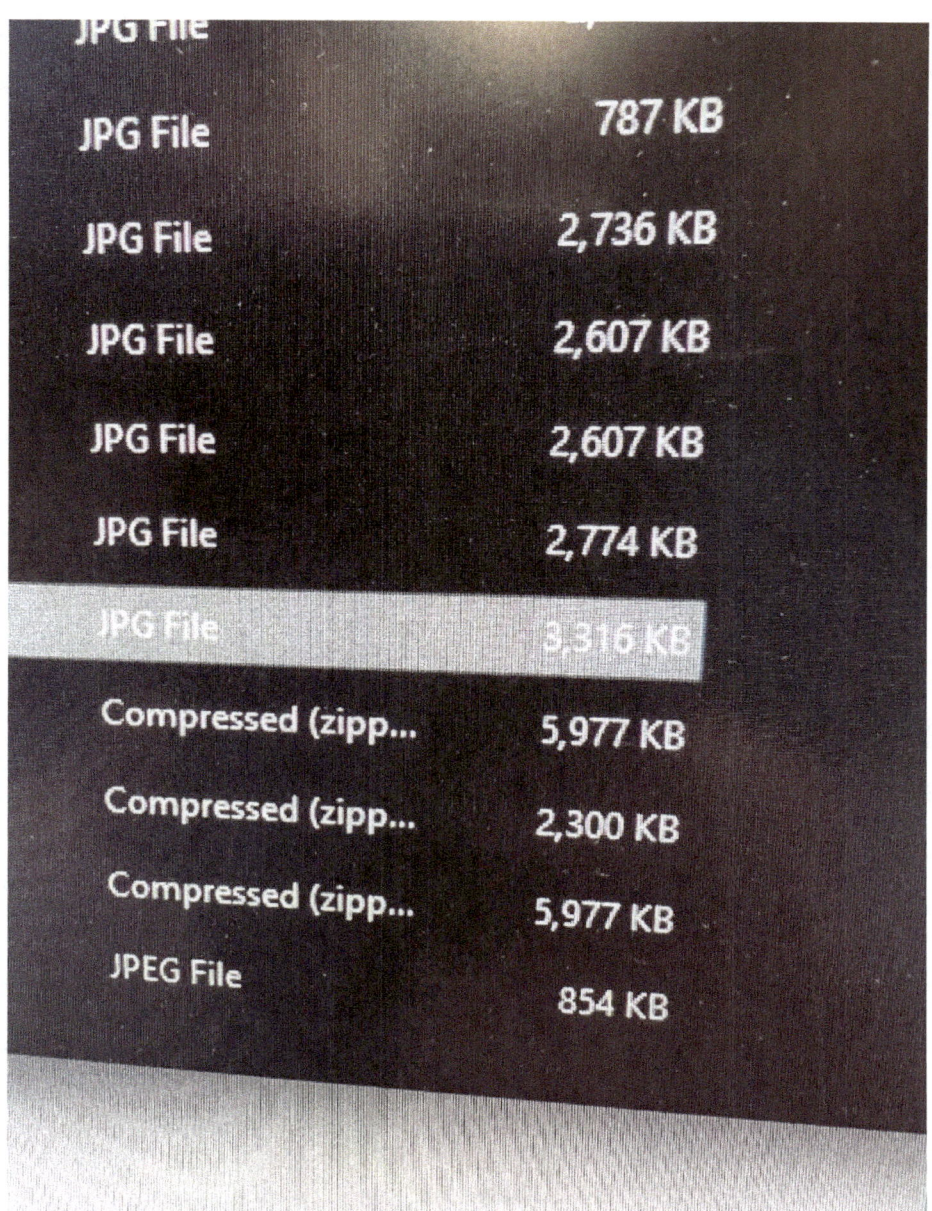

Figure 7-6: This file was 3316 KB

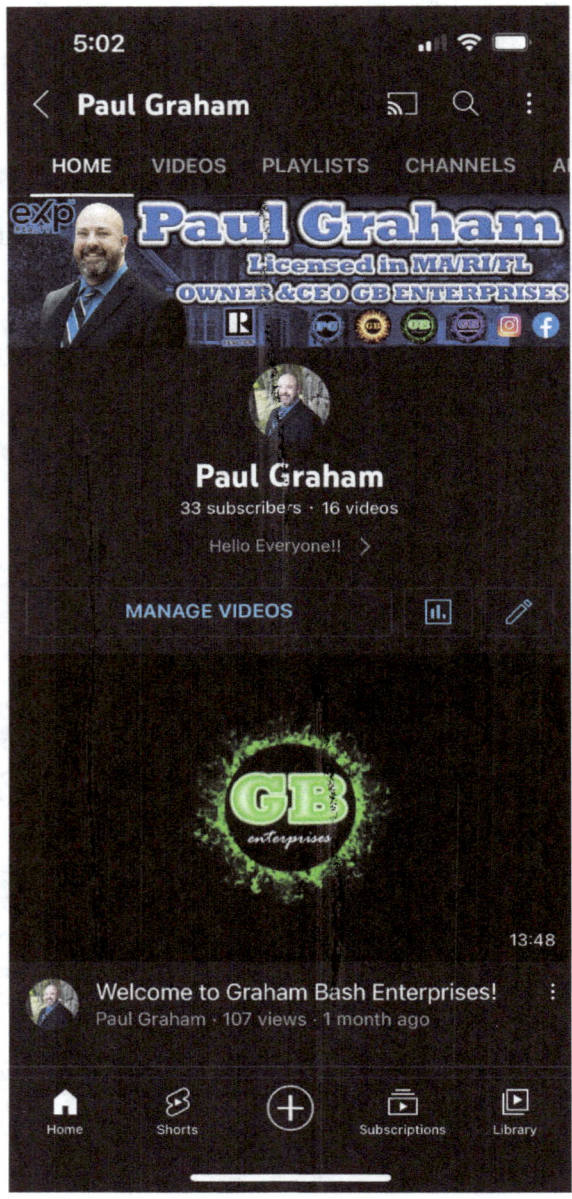

Figure 7-7: On my YouTube channel when I was starting out, I randomly check it and its 33 subscribers 16 videos

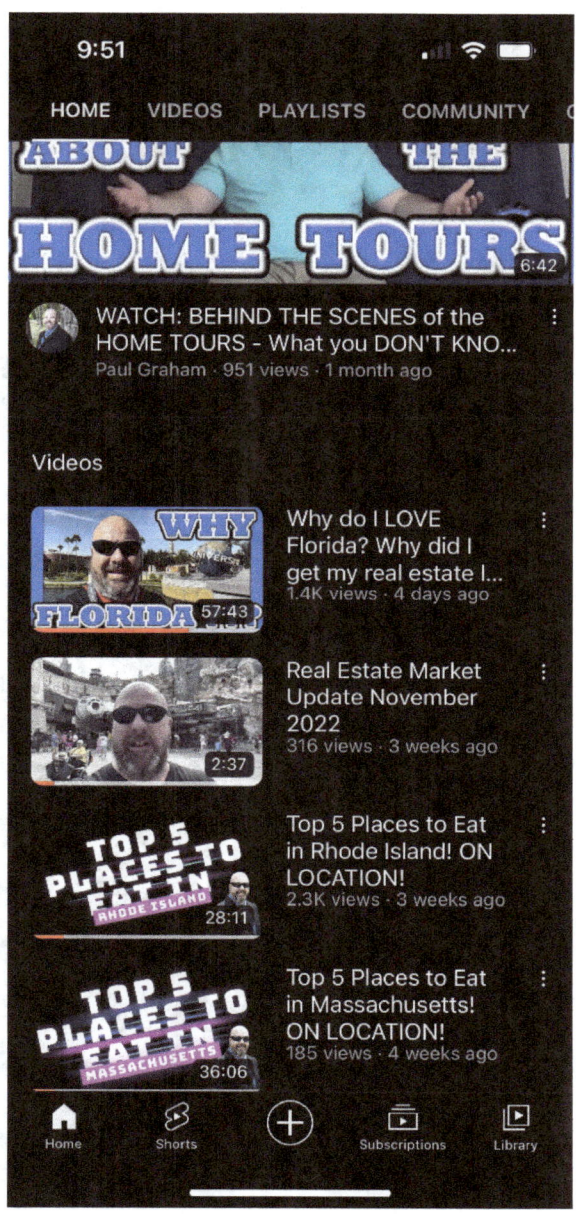

Figure 7-8: This Real Estate Market Update November randomly had 316 views when I checked it

Figure 7-9: My Hometown video randomly had 316 views when I checked it

After the second time of checking on the views for my videos and seeing 316 again, I'm like you've got to be kidding me with this 316 stuff! Some people probably think I'm overthinking it now, but these little moments are standing out to me. And they are occurring at a time in my life that is highly questionable. I'm starting a new venture that I have no experience in. Being on commission is unlike anything I've ever done. I've always had jobs that have set incomes. I've always been a planner. I needed these little signs to guide and keep me on track mentally that I was doing the right thing. That I was on the right path.

Here's a few more:

Figure 7:10: I'm learning how to fly my drone, I'm watching this video and I keep looking at this storage at the bottom of 03:11:16. Not exactly 3:16, but close enough to grab my attention.

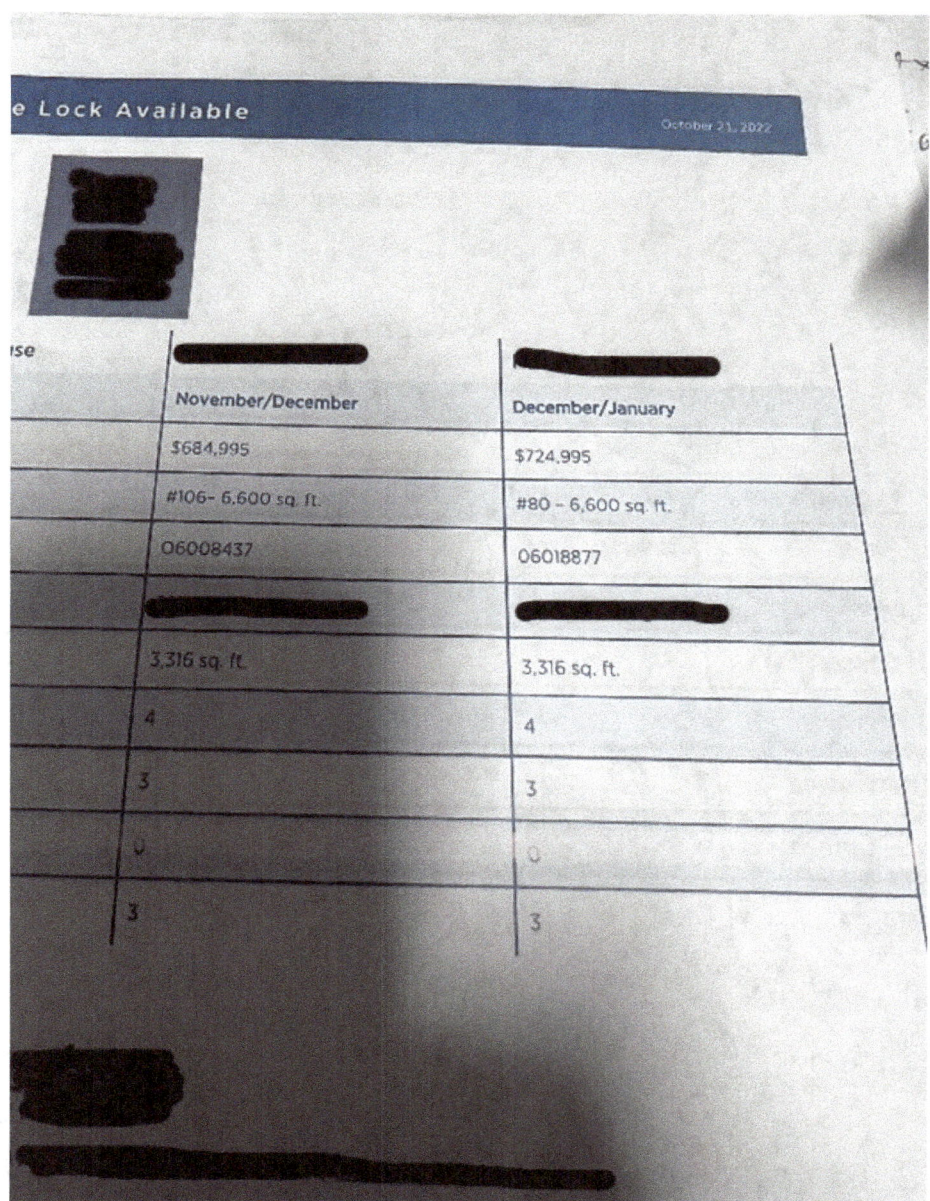

e Lock Available	October 21, 2022

	November/December	December/January
	$684,995	$724,995
	#106– 6,600 sq. ft.	#80 – 6,600 sq. ft.
	06008437	06018877
	3,316 sq. ft.	3,316 sq. ft.
	4	4
	3	3
	0	0
	3	3

Figure 7-11: I'm looking through the brochure pamphlet on this property I just conducted a video tour for and its 3316 SQ Ft

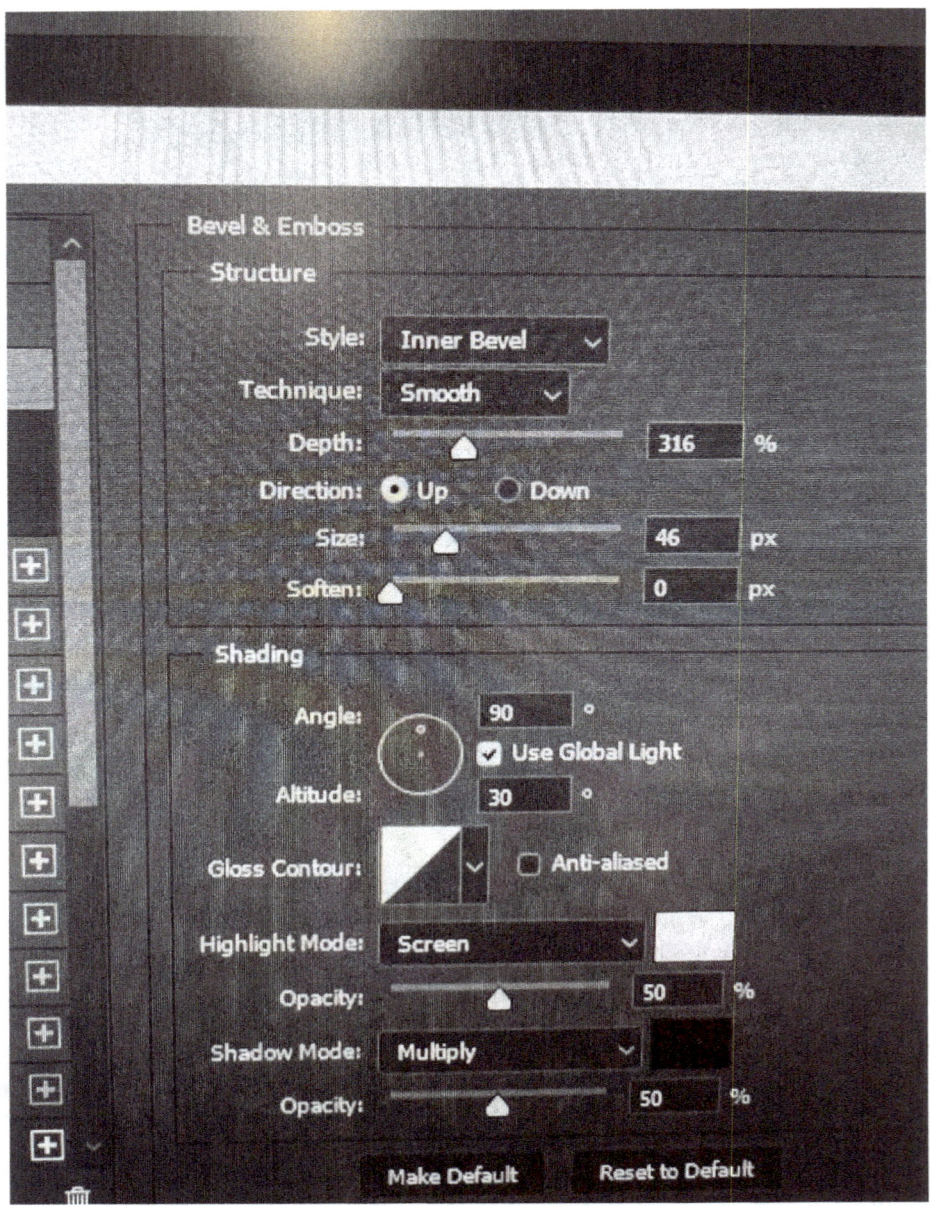

Figure 7-12: There is another bevel depth on my logo that is perfectly what I am looking for and it's 316%

Some people may look at this and say ok c'mon man, you are taking this to the extreme level. I could probably find a similar combination of numbers over and over if I'm trying to see it. And that may be entirely true. Maybe the odds of seeing these are not as great as I am perceiving them. Maybe I'm subconsciously looking for 316 now. Maybe. But one thing I know is that every time I see 316 now, it fuels me to believe that whatever path I'm on, this is the right path to be on right now. It gives me a sense of calm.

And my whole life was definitely not like this. Most of the 316 events were spread out over many, many years and occurring at very particular moments. All of these real estate signs have been over the course of 1 year or less.

CHAPTER 8
Our Two Miracles

O ne thing I wanted to touch on before this book concludes is our two little miracles. One of the things I've always envisioned when I was growing up was having my own family one day. I loved my family and wanted to keep their memories alive and continue family traditions for the next generation. I loved my parents so much that I couldn't wait to be parents of my own children one day.

In early conversations with my wife before she was my wife, she had the same goals and desires. She always wanted to be a mother and have a family. That's part of what made our match together such a great one.

One thing that threw a monkey wrench into the whole plan is

that we struggled with infertility. We tried for many years to have children. Sometimes we tried hard, some years we forgot about it and just said if it happens, it happens and just didn't worry about it. We said that but I'm sure in the back of both of our minds we were still disappointed that it never happened.

We really wanted our own biological children, but we mainly just wanted to have and raise children. We started looking into adoption. But adoption was extremely expensive. We thought it would be easy to adopt a possibly unwanted baby. But there were no services that we found like this. All of the adoption services we found were extremely expensive and out of our budget means.

Every home that we lived in after we were married, we always had a "Hopefully future baby's room" where we would store items for if we ever had a baby. At times it became a storage area with just a few totes with baby type items or family heirlooms we wanted to pass along.

Eventually, we went to see an infertility specialist. We went through a variety of tests, tried a couple procedures and they did not work. My wife was devastated. My attitude was that I was down about it, but also thought - Hey we haven't lost anything. We didn't have children before this attempt and just because it didn't work, nothing has really changed, we are in the same boat we were in before.

But my wife did not see it that way. She saw it as her body was letting us down. And there were concerning test results on my end that made me remind her that her body was not the reason that led to us struggling naturally. But she just saw it as once it was up to her body to do its part, it was not doing what it was supposed to be doing. It was very emotional for her. Especially during the waiting period to see if it actually worked. It was just an emotional roller coaster for her and then to get the bad news that it did not work just devastated her each time.

So, after trying this method a couple of times, we decided to take a break from trying these procedures and just relax for a while and see what happens. A few years went by, and we now were approaching 10 years of trying. Some of those years really trying, some just seeing what happens. But during this time my wife is very sensitive to the subject of pregnancies and others having babies. It was so emotionally difficult to see other people having babies with such ease and for us it was such a struggle. Everyone would tell us, don't worry. It will happen one day. But you don't know that it will. You don't. So, if someone you know is going through that, I would not suggest telling them that. It does not help.

At my career, which was corrections at this point in my life, open enrollment came up for healthcare. I just randomly saw one day around this time frame, an article with the top healthcare facilities in the nation. I saw that Boston, Massachusetts was the home of some of the top healthcare facilities in the entire nation. Massachusetts General Hospital was ranked number 1 and Brigham and Women's was ranked number 4 or something like that at the time.

It totally changed my outlook on healthcare. Yeah, I wasn't right next door to Boston, but the facilities were a reasonable driving distance, especially when considering that they were regarded as the top ones in the nation. I mean they were right here in my home state! As you get older, you start to think things might go wrong health wise. Especially with seeing what happened with my mom, my father-in-law, and just other people I have met in life along the way. I wasn't even thinking about the infertility piece yet, just general healthcare. So, I switched insurances during the open enrollment, I selected plans that included the great Boston healthcare facilities. I switched my doctors to this network.

I was loving my decision. I immediately felt like they were more thorough than my current medical network was. The travel to Boston was not even that big of a deal, I figured out the best times to avoid the traffic and scheduled my appointments for then. Quincy Market, which has a wide variety of food options, is walking distance from my primary care provider's office. So, the once or twice a year that I have to travel there, I make it worth the trip and stop by Quincy Market.

My wife also switches to the network as well. She chooses Brigham and Women's. I choose Mass General. We figure we can see how each one is and then decide if one of us wants to switch over. The good news for today is that they combined networks and are now one network but back then, they were separate.

We started talking about infertility again. Do we want to give it another try now that we are in the Boston healthcare networks?

She's nervous about going through the emotions of it all again, but ultimately, we decide ok let's schedule a visit and see what happens. We meet with the doctor. He sends us for even more testing this time. They are very, very thorough before any procedures or anything like that are scheduled.

Once we started the procedure process, let me tell you, there was a lot more to it than we could have imagined. There were points we had to go every other morning and then every morning and had to be there for 7am. In Boston. In rush hour. Both of us worked until 11pm, luckily for me it was before forced overtime was reigning supreme there. So, we would get out at 11pm, quickly get home and to sleep and then get up super early to be there on time. There was no changing the time, this was the timeframe the facilities set aside for the infertility patients in these labs and ultrasound rooms.

So not only was this mentally draining, but it was also physically draining. During the process, we found out that we could go to a closer facility on certain days of the week, but even that one was 45 minutes away or so. At one point we went 10 or 11 mornings in a row.

So, we went to all of these appointments, had the procedure done and were now in the waiting game to see the results. My wife gets emotional again. This was probably about a 6- or 7-month process and here we go, fingers crossed, prayers said. The day comes to receive the phone call with the results. We get the call "Sorry, it didn't work this time". We had been down this road before. My wife is devastated. I'm down and out about it but also trying to stay positive, especially for her. I try to look at it through the positive eyes like last time, thinking well it just wasn't meant to be yet. Nothing has really changed. We didn't have a baby before, we don't have one now. Those concepts didn't really help her too much, she was just emotionally drained again and felt like it was probably never going to happen.

So, the office asks us if we want to try again. We tell them we need a break, and we will contact them when we are ready. We just put the whole idea on the backburner for now and try to get back to normalcy in our lives.

That happened in June, it is now September, and we are at a funeral service for my aunt's sister. We are in the cemetery and come back to the car and we have a missed call from the Boston hospital that we had the procedure done at. Just very odd timing. My wife listens to the voicemail, and they are calling saying that we were approved to do another procedure. Our initial reaction was – Are they even calling the right person? We never requested to be approved for anything and our last conversation with them was back in June saying we will contact them when we are ready.

My wife and I are not even really thinking about it right now. It has not been that long since all of those early morning daily visits to Boston and the whole emotional process of doing the procedure and awaiting the results. At this point in our life, we had tried procedures three times all with the same results. We were just not ready mentally to go through all of that again.

But us taking things as signs the way we do after these 316 experiences (I got my wife noticing things now). We start to ask ourselves about it. What are the odds that we get this phone call while we are at the cemetery for this funeral service? What if it's a sign from my aunt's sister to do this procedure? This lady was such a sweet person also. She always attended our annual bash and was always so pleasant to be around. She and her husband were just great people.

We really were not ready and if it wasn't at this exact point that we received the call, we probably would have said not yet. But because we felt like maybe, just maybe, even no matter how small of a percentage chance that there was something to the fact that this call happened at the exact moment we were at this funeral service - The few moments we were out of the car, we discuss it. After discussing it, we ultimately decide maybe we should just do it. We're not really into it mentally, but let's take another chance with it because of the sign thing and just see what happens.

So, we called them back and asked if the message was even meant for us. They tell us it was, so we tell them we want to do it. This time is a little different. We are kind of just going through the motions with it. Our expectations are not high, we are just going with the flow. We are kind of numb to the whole idea of going through this again. So, we do all the tests, do all the early morning appointments again while working late the nights before. We get to the day where everything is aligned just right to schedule the procedure. The doctor tells us it will be the following day which will be Halloween.

My first reaction is that I can't call out sick on Halloween. At my correction officer job, it is an unwritten rule to never call out on holiday or day like that. It's just common courtesy to your fellow officers because if you call out it could cause someone else to have to stay for mandatory overtime in your place. The mindset is - What makes your family more important than their family? Now if you call out on regular day, it happens, people get sick, have doctors' appointments, etc. But if you can avoid calling out a significant family day, you should avoid it at all costs.

Obviously, this was a significant event for us, but If I could avoid it, I would want to. I tell my wife, "Can you ask them if they can do it on the next day, November 1st?" My wife immediately counters back "They can't change the day. Everything is ready to do it tomorrow." I say, "Can you just ask? That's all I'm asking is if they can do it the following day, if that will jeopardize anything?" My wife reluctantly asks. "Sure" they tell her, "That is not a problem and won't affect anything". So here we go, it's now scheduled for November 1st.

We get to the appointment and my wife starts to tell me she doesn't want us to get our hopes up, she doesn't want to get too excited about it. I interrupted her and immediately blurt out "It's going to work this time". She gives me a look and says, "What did I just say?". I said, "I know, and I think it's going to work this time.". She shakes her head because I completely disregarded what she was saying.

So we go into the room, and they complete the procedure. I tell her to just relax and not to worry about it. Once everything is done, we go home and now it's just the waiting game. Did it work? Did it not work? It's about 2 weeks before you find out.

So, we try not to get our hopes up. My wife is going through the emotions, but it's not as tough this time as the previous times although still nerve racking. We go to the various tests and different things. We finally get to the long-awaited day where we are just awaiting the phone call with the results. We are sitting around, getting antsy. I tell my wife, let's go to the 99 Restaurant, take our mind off things. If we get a positive call while we are out, it can turn into a celebration meal. If we get negative news, it can be a cheer us up meal.

We are driving down the road and she's getting impatient. "I'm going to call", she says. So, she calls the number we have on file. They tell her she should be getting a call by Monday (which was a couple of days away). My wife, immediately upset, tells her "I can't wait until Monday, this is like torture." As she is having this conversation, another Boston number starts beeping in on the other line. She tells this current person, "I'm getting another call, hold on one second". She switches to the other line. I'm just driving along in the meantime, trying to be as observant and nosy as I can as to her conversations.

All of the sudden, tears start coming down her face. The news could be going either way at this point. I'm trying to glance over at her to get a feel for her emotions. Her tears don't look like sad tears, they look like happy tears. I hear her asking "Are you sure you have the right number? Are you sure this is for me?" I immediately knew the good news! It worked! I couldn't believe it fully! I thought it was going to work whether it was from the funeral sign or what not, but with all of the past results, I wasn't totally sure. I also questioned myself as to requesting them to change the date of the procedure. That could make all the difference in the timing of the placement of it working perfectly or not working at all.

It's the happiest phone call we'll probably ever get in our lives! But the news gets better. As we go through the process of tests and eventually an ultrasound, we find out one more thing. Not just one baby but twins! Instant family. It was just so exhilarating and exciting! After everything we went through for over 10 years and to finally have children, it was just unbelievable. It was definitely a miracle to us - two miracles actually! We're probably going to spoil them too much because we just tried so hard to have them for so long and they are just so special to us. They completed our lives.

A few fun facts I wanted to throw in there on these miracles. One was the day of the delivery. It was still a little nerve racking because so many things could still go wrong. You never truly stop worrying during the whole pregnancy, during the delivery, and probably will be worrying for the rest of our lives. But things went relatively smoothly at first. Our daughter came out first, she was in position and ready to go. Then our son didn't seem ready to leave.

They had to fight and pull him out. Watching the urgency of the delivery doctor definitely made me nervous as they were trying to get him out. When they did get him out, it was just such a relief. They were born early and needed to be in the NICU (Newborn Intensive Care Unit) but they both turned out to be very healthy. Such a blessing and miracle!

The first fun fact is the doctor who delivered our miracle twins was Dr. Easter. It was the first time we met her. My wife's regular doctor never made it there for whatever reason. It was probably the timing of everything as my wife went from not in labor to in labor really fast there. But we took that as a little sign because if you are familiar at all with the Bible, you've probably heard the story of Easter, with the rise of Christ and everything that came along with that. For the delivery doctor's name to be Easter was just another shake our heads in awe type of moment.

The second fun fact is that after a few days in the Boston NICU, they were strong enough to be transferred to a local NICU closer to us. The date they arrived there was on the 3rd of the month and they stayed there in that NICU an additional 16 days before being discharged, both on the same day. Initially I didn't notice this fun fact, it was not until later when going over medical history with medical providers when we continuously were asked how long they were in the NICU for. The 3:16 was right there in front of me, but I never put it together until we were asked these medical questions later on.

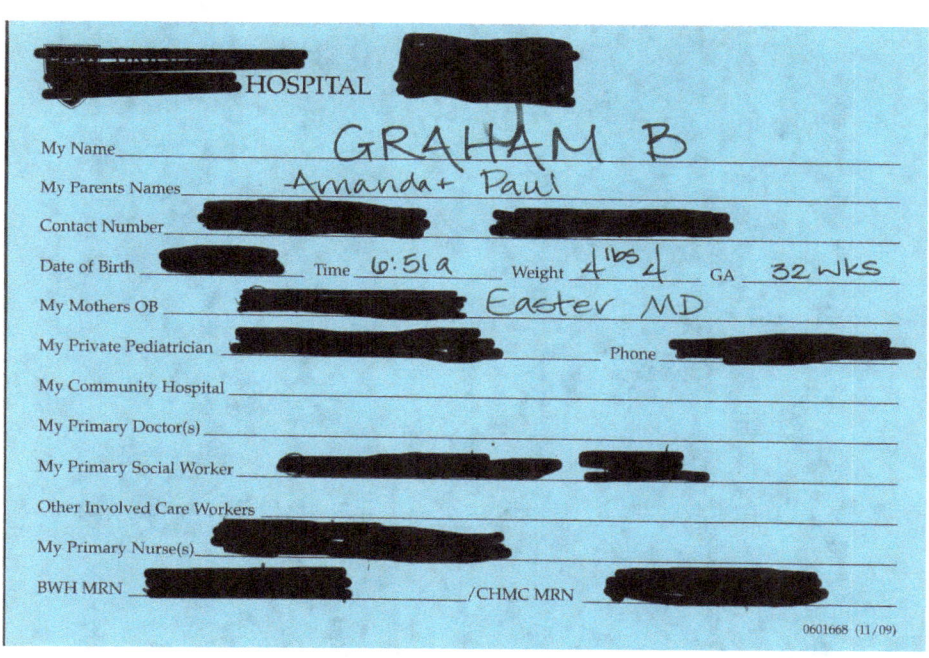

Figure 8-1: Birth Card in the NICU that showed Dr. Easter

Then the last fun fact is that I kept seeing this body temperature or whatever this number even was, on the screen over my son's incubator in the NICU. It kept sticking out like a sore thumb, so I finally just had to snap a photo of it.

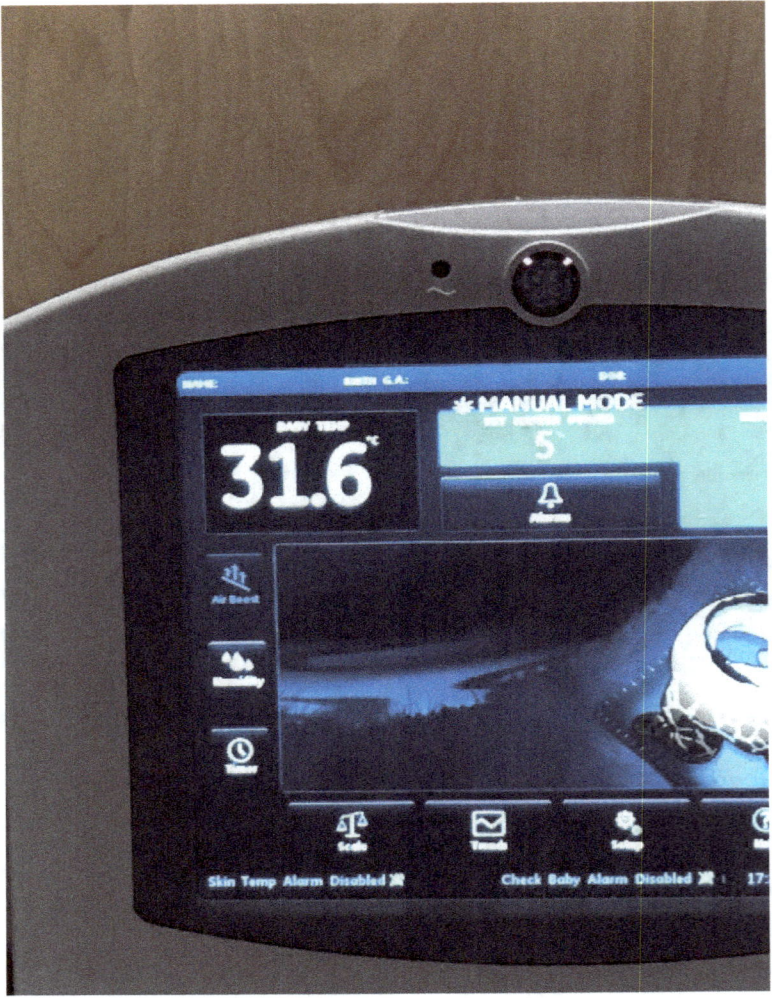

Figure 8-2: 31.6 degrees Baby Temp

CHAPTER 9
Why I Truly Believe

These signs I've seen over the years definitely guide me and point me in the direction of believing. I mean there are just too many of them happening at precise moments in my life for me to say they are just coincidences. Thinking of them keeps me on track if I ever start to drift off. But what has truly made me believe is the combination of these signs along with learning about God.

One movie/documentary I watched by Lee Strobel – "The Case for a Creator", really sealed the deal for me with how I view everything now. It is a book he wrote, but the film is what brings it to life for me. The story of Lee Strobel is that he was an atheist journalist whose wife began getting involved in a church. Lee went on a quest to investigate the validity of the Christian Faith and thought he was going to uncover why it was not true. But his investigation took him to an alternate destination. He ended up seeing so much evidence that Christianity was true that he became a Christian. A lot of the information he revealed really got me thinking.

In High School, I was similar to Lee in the fact that science is what made me question the realness of God. Was he really real? Evolution seemed to provide a logical pathway for how we became humans. But does it really? Now I started to question some things about it. How are there so many different species? How did life evolve to that many different forms? Did the environment on Earth really change that many times? When it did change for survival of the fittest, why did the "unfit" species still survive creating the vast number of species we still have today? Where are the "gaps" in the tree of life or the "in between" species? Why are they so different from insects to elephants to birds to snakes to bacteria to humans, I could go on and on.

In "The Case for a Creator", what really got me thinking was the complexity of life. They showed an animated model of the Bacterial Flagellum. They broke down all of its moving parts. A propeller, a rotor, hook, driveshaft. Biochemist Michael J Behe said "That's an outboard motor. That's designed. That's no chance assembly of parts."

I started thinking about how complex the human body is. All of the cells and parts that make up a human body. The eyes, the brain, the way we can eat food and break it down into usable molecules. All of the organs and how they all work together in a system. How could any species, let alone a tiny organism, no matter how long it had time to try, ever evolve into this? How could each of these parts have first been formed through years of change? How was DNA first evolved into? The more I really thought about things, the more I really started wondering how evolution could have really happened.

What is even more seemingly crazy to me is the idea of how many parts go into creating a human being like we just talked about from the DNA to the cells, on and on. Then you throw in the fact that not only can this human being be created, but they have a way to reproduce themselves and make another one. How can that system be tweaked or created during evolution or "chance by natural selection". The more and more I thought about it, the more and more I see a designer. A creator.

Look at a car. Look at all of the parts that make up a car – the engine, the tires, the doors, the brakes, the steering wheel, everything that goes into it. What are the odds that a car could just come from nothing or be created by "chance" over millions of years? No, someone designed and created that car. And living organisms are so much more complex than a car.

To me it takes more faith to believe in Evolution than it does to believe in a Creator. The Ironic part that I share with Lee Strobel is that I went from science causing me to question the existence of God to science now being the reason I do believe in God. The more science I see, the more I see us learning about our Creator.

I used to think God was not logically possible. But think about your world right now. Close your eyes and think about it. Either think of or forget the research of our world both past and present. Just think of how it is RIGHT now. What is around you? How logically possible is the Sun? A big burning ball of fire that never goes out. Also, in a location that is the exact perfect distance from the Earth to sustain life as we know it. Now think about gravity, and the planets orbiting around this sun, how it all works. How logically possible is it for that to exist? Then we have all of these different things in the world that we deem "alive" that have lungs, hearts, eyes and all of these organs and systems that work together. All of these things occurred naturally and by chance? How is this anymore logically possible then there being a creator out there somewhere?

Just look at plant life. Depending on where you live but when winter changes to spring, something almost magical happens. Let's take the month of March for example in New England. There can be cold days, there could be warm days. Each day can be different. If you look at the grass in your yard and the leaves on the trees or lack thereof. Each day can go by in March and your lawn does not grow, the leaves do not bud. Day after Day, you go out into the yard, and nothing is happening with these things. You can introduce water into the equation. It can rain and rain and rain. Still nothing. The Sun is out and shining brightly each day. Nothing. But as soon as it gets just a tad warmer out and you introduce just the right set of circumstances. Boom. Everything starts blooming and growing.

I get it. There's physics, chemistry, biology, etc. There are all these areas of science that have explanations for certain things. Just because you can explain how these things happen, doesn't mean it's still not amazing that we live in a universe where they *do* happen. There are two major explanation sides in this: Creation and Science. Sometimes you just have to forget both sides of it for a minute and just look at the "wow" of everything and ask yourself how possible this stuff came to be is. One thing I always found fascinating was that when a non-believer doesn't understand the answer to something, they answer "Science". When a believer doesn't understand the answer to something they say the reason is "God". What if the two are actually in essence the same thing?

And now to tie Jesus into it. Jesus is not just in the Bible; he is also recognized in other historical documents as being someone who actually did live. I sometimes wonder, why do people believe so much in him? Why did people follow him? Were these just made-up stories that got passed down generation to generation? Why would people still believe it all these years later?

People saw him alive. People saw him perform these miracles. The world was different back then, but was it? Do you think people were just gullible and just believed fairytale stories? No, there was probably just as much skepticism in the world then as there is today. I mean, look at what the Romans did to Jesus. A lot of people were skeptical of him. A lot of people didn't see any of these miracles and did not believe he did those things.

If you heard today that some guy just cured someone who was blind, would you believe it? No! Would you follow him? No! Now if you were there and you saw this, would you believe it? Maybe. What if you actually knew this person who was blind and now saw that he was in fact cured? Now would you believe? Yes, probably! Would you follow this miracle performer? Maybe. Let's say you now heard he performed some other miracle, would you be more apt to believe it? Probably.

Now let's say you weren't there but someone you trusted very much who never lied to you, told you they were there and witnessed one of these miracles, would you believe it? Good possibility.

Witnesses saw Jesus alive after he died. If that's not the craziest story you ever heard, I'm not sure what would be. If you lived in that era, or any era, for you to believe that either you had to see it for yourself or definitely have a lot of trust in the person that told you they saw it.

As crazy as this story was, it lived on. For that story to live on, enough people heard it from someone they trusted to believe it. This story kept getting passed on from someone that was trusted to someone else who was trusted to someone else who was trusted and so on, so much so that now over 2000 years later, the stories are still alive and followed. It's tough to comprehend now because now it has been so many years, so you personally cannot relate as well to people that were there. But for this ball to get rolling as big and fast as it got with the number of Christians in the world today, it most likely had to have started from some truth. Or else it probably would never have grown into what it has become. That is where the word faith comes into the picture. Having faith that what all of these people saw before you came from some sort of truth. And it wasn't just 2000 years of storytelling, these events were recorded in writing, within a lifetime of them happening, and were based on witness testimony.

It's very difficult to believe in something, truly believe in something unless you see it yourself. I know, I'm one of those people. I struggled with my faith on and off for years. But faith is an important word there. You don't have all the answers, you don't know everything. You have to put your faith in something. Whether you are putting your faith in the science and the evolution side of it that things happened by "chance". Or if you are putting your faith in God or at least a creator if you are not there yet. Either way you are taking a leap of faith. Which one is a bigger leap?

JUST A THEORY

This is just a theory that I had. It's not in the Bible, I have no idea if it's true or remotely close to true. I'm not saying I believe it to be exactly how it works. So, if you want to skip this whole chapter feel free. I just figured I would mention it, because the concept of it interested me enough to keep it in my thoughts.

One of the biggest things that I struggled with when thinking of God was why do bad things happen to good people? Why does someone get raped? Why does someone get murdered? Why do bad things happen to children? Why do these unbelievable cruel things happen in a world that a supposed God is overseeing? Why does he allow this stuff to happen?

One day this thought just popped into my head, like I said, right or wrong, this is what I was thinking about. Take eternity. Eternity. I can't even comprehend eternity. That's one of the limits of the human brain. It's so difficult to comprehend that something has no beginning and no end. Everything we see whether it's a person, a book, a movie, a structure, a company, a tree, a piece of fruit, your pet dog or cat, something constructed like a house or manufactured like an automobile. They all have a beginning, and most have an ending. If there is no ending yet, in your mind there will eventually be an ending to it (old structure, company that is in business now).

It's so difficult to believe something just always was or always will be. Whether you believe in God and science or just science, it is still a struggle wondering how the universe always was and how it will always be. And if you believe the universe did begin, how did it begin? What was before that? Even if nothing, that still seems like something.

At one point in my life, I just wondered if everything was just on a big loop like a circle and time would just repeat itself over billions of years and so on. But if that was true, still where did the circle come from? So that idea probably is not how it was. Then I thought differently. I thought of Infinity as just being some straight line that we just cannot comprehend.

Infinity, a tough thing to conceive, but let's just draw a straight line of time for example and say that it is the infinity of the universe:

Infinity

Now let's think again about the horrors of the world and why do they happen. What if our time on earth is where we learn what good and evil is? Maybe we need to see evil so we can understand it which also helps us understand good.

To truly understand evil, we need to see it, experience it, be hurt by it. That is the only way we will truly know what it is. Maybe that's part of why we have to go through so many hardships in life.

But why is it not fair? Why does this particular person have to be murdered or raped so that this other person can see it or be affected by it? I don't know.

Maybe God has a plan for that. Let's examine the line of Infinity again. Try to imagine real Infinity where this line just continues on and on and on. This circle represents someone's life on earth in the grand scheme of Infinity. It's just a tiny blip on the radar. A needle in a haystack. Probably even smaller. As crazy as this sounds maybe God will use a victim of even the worst of crimes to show and teach us what pure evil looks like, if this pain that this victim went through is just a tiny, tiny blip on the radar in the grand scheme of things. What if the victim of the evil would be rewarded 10 fold or more and that in the grand scheme of time and infinity it's such a miniscule moment and the victim totally understands later why they had to go through that and they are completely ok with it.

Infinity

I know this sounds crazy and I'm not saying I believe it. I try to mentally make sense of why the evil in this world happens. Because let's face it whether you believe this theory or you don't, these horrific crimes still happen in the world to undeserving victims. Maybe Satan, also known as the devil, causes these things. The truth is I don't know. I don't know why bad things happen to good people. And I will probably never know while I'm on this earth. But hopefully one day I'll be standing next to God in Heaven, and I will be looking down at this world and I will be saying, "Oooh, that's why this happens the way it does. I get it now. Now I understand.". It will be like the end of good mystery novel.

I don't think a loving God would want anyone to go through some of these things, let alone children. So, I feel like there is some reason why all this stuff happens – a reason we may never get the answer to. But I would like to believe that it does serve some sought of purpose.

I have a tough time wrapping my head around the fact that a loving God would allow anyone to go through this if there was no purpose behind it. Maybe that purpose is to truly see and experience evil. Maybe there are other reasons why these horrific things happen. Maybe it is as simple as allowing free-will. I'm sure there are a million different theories out there, one of which may be the accurate one.

CONCLUSION:

sometimes reflect back on that day that I planned on taking my own life. I think about how stupid and dumb that would have been. I think about EVERYTHING I would have missed out on that happened after that day – The fun times with my friends, fun times with my family, meeting my spouse, starting a family. MY CHILDREN!!!!!!!!!! They would have never been born. It's just crazy to me how much I would have thrown away by completing that decision. A lifetime of happiness with fun gatherings, vacations, etc. It's just insane.

In this world, we want things FAST. We don't want to wait for things to develop. In high school, I wanted a girlfriend FAST. Our concept of how time works and what FAST really means is off a lot of the time. I didn't want to wait a couple of years or a few years. That to me felt like eternity back then.

Looking back at it now, a couple of years WERE FAST relatively speaking. It seems like the whole era of meeting my spouse and getting married was a snap of the fingers, the blink of an eye.

It's a battle I think that is ongoing even with this knowledge. I think about things I'm going through now and think some things are not happening fast enough. I think about the next 20 years of my life, God willing if I make it that far, and I think that it will be a long time from now. But truth is, fast forward my life 20 years from now and I'll be looking back at the era that I am in now as the blink of an eye, a snap of the fingers.

To get through hard times, you have to understand the magnitude and the actual length of time and how long things take. All too many times we get caught up in the moment and the moment ends up being less and less significant as time goes along. How many times in life have you reflected back and said, wow I'm actually happy that didn't work out the way I originally wanted it to or else I may have never had this happen or met this person or went down this whole journey in life. Sometimes we just have to have a little faith that things are working out the way that will be best for us in the long run. Maybe, just maybe there is someone out there who knows what is best in the future and is helping to guide your life.

That concept is not always easy to have. I've been very fortunate and blessed in my journey with seeing so many 3:16 signs and it just kept me close to God and praying. The closer I feel to him, the closer I feel that I am on the right track even if I can't imagine the finish line yet. 3:16 has just played such a tremendous role in my life. I felt like I should share it with people.

My goal with this book is to just share my thoughts and personal experiences with you. You might believe me, you might not, you might think I'm crazy, you might think I'll make anything into a sign. I understand that. I've always been a skeptical person in my life as well. The way the world has been going, the more and more skepticism is out there. People challenge things that were just accepted before like landing on the moon, the earth is round, all the government conspiracy theories, there are just so many things now that are questioned. So, if you are questioning me and what I've seen, I totally understand.

My hope is that if you get past that stuff that you can take a moment to think about some of the things in this book. Maybe you can investigate some of the concepts yourself. I don't claim to be an expert by any stretch of the imagination. I just happened to notice some signs and put some stuff together. But I'll tell you what did happen. I became a true believer. I started off unsure, but now I truly do believe.

I'm not trying to paint myself as a weekly church goer my whole life or even now. I do attend more now in my life, but there have been times where I have been consistently attending and then other phases where I don't go for months at a time. I have to say though that I always do feel better when I go often. I feel closer to God. It is especially great when you find a church that not only teaches you and inspires you but is also fun and entertaining to attend with great music and a great atmosphere. I'm lucky that I stumbled upon the one I am attending now.

I know a lot of these 3:16 instances highlight negative times in my life and that's probably no coincidence either, but I could also write a whole book much longer than this focusing on all of the positive experiences in my life. My life overall has been filled with so much joy and I have had so much fun living it. The people I've met, the family members I have, my spouse, our children – it's just been a tremendous journey and I've loved sharing it with everyone.

I could have written chapters for many more people in my life. My life has been influenced by so many people. I have great relationships with additional close friends and family members, ex co-workers. I have cousins that I am close to. One cousin I lived next door to all throughout my childhood and spent so much time together. I have another cousin who I am very close with, we call each other "bro-cuz" because he is like a brother. We didn't live next door, but we still spent a lot of our childhood and school vacations together. I was very honored to be the best man at his wedding. My brothers could have easily had a chapter each on how much we mean to each other and how important they are to my life. My wife, the love of my life, could have her own chapter without question. But when you dive into who has chapters and why, you might not want to be in one of the chapters, at least not for a long time.

I wrote this book for a few different groups of people. I wrote it for people that already believe that might think it's cool to hear about some of these signs. Maybe it fuels their enthusiasm like it does mine. I wrote it for people who do want to believe and struggle with believing it is really real. I wrote it for someone that does not believe but maybe sees the signs I've seen and maybe it makes them just think about it a little bit more.

And perhaps the most important group of people I wrote it for is for anyone who has struggled with depressing thoughts and has been in that dark place questioning if you even want to live in this world anymore. The advice I give that person is to just give it some time. Even if it is one more day. I used to tell myself that at times. If I got into a dark place with dark thoughts, I would take a deep breath and say to myself "Just give it one more day and see how you feel tomorrow". Most times, the next day, you feel a little bit better about the situation. Not all situations only take a day overall to get past, but I always felt giving it one more day really helped me get through some tough times. You don't know the future until you get there, but once I did get there, I almost wanted to go back in time and smack myself for thinking what I was thinking. At the time I didn't see it that way, but now I see everything I would have lost out on. It far outweighs what I thought I was missing out on or feeling hopeless about back then.

That's why I decided to share all of these personal stories with you. I struggled internally between writing this book or just keeping these stories to my own personal self and family. But if it could help even just one person possibly think twice about their decisions, whether it was dark thoughts they were having, or whether to put your faith to believe in God or Jesus or even just think about believing a little bit more, it would be worth taking the time to put this out there.

Thank you for taking the time to read this book. I'm going to close with some personal photographs of different things. But I also want to close in the same way I closed my eulogy about my uncle Bob:

"As Pastor also said - If I'm wrong about heaven and hell and you're right, what happens? I really have nothing to lose. We all end up in the ground anyway big deal.

But if I'm right and you're wrong, you have everything to lose. Think about that for a minute. What if you're wrong? So I would say - at-least do your research and try to find out for yourself the truth. Don't go by what you always believed or what your parents believed or even what I'm telling you I believe. Go find out for yourself. Challenge yourself and go where the journey takes you. Have an open mind and open heart. It's the most important journey Bob would want you to go on before your last day comes."

Is this all really real?

Figure 9-1: Me and Rafal at his wedding

Figure 9-2: Me at Daytona Beach where I heard Rafal say
he believed in God

Figure 9-3 and Figure 9-4: Me and Rafal at
Daytona International Speedway

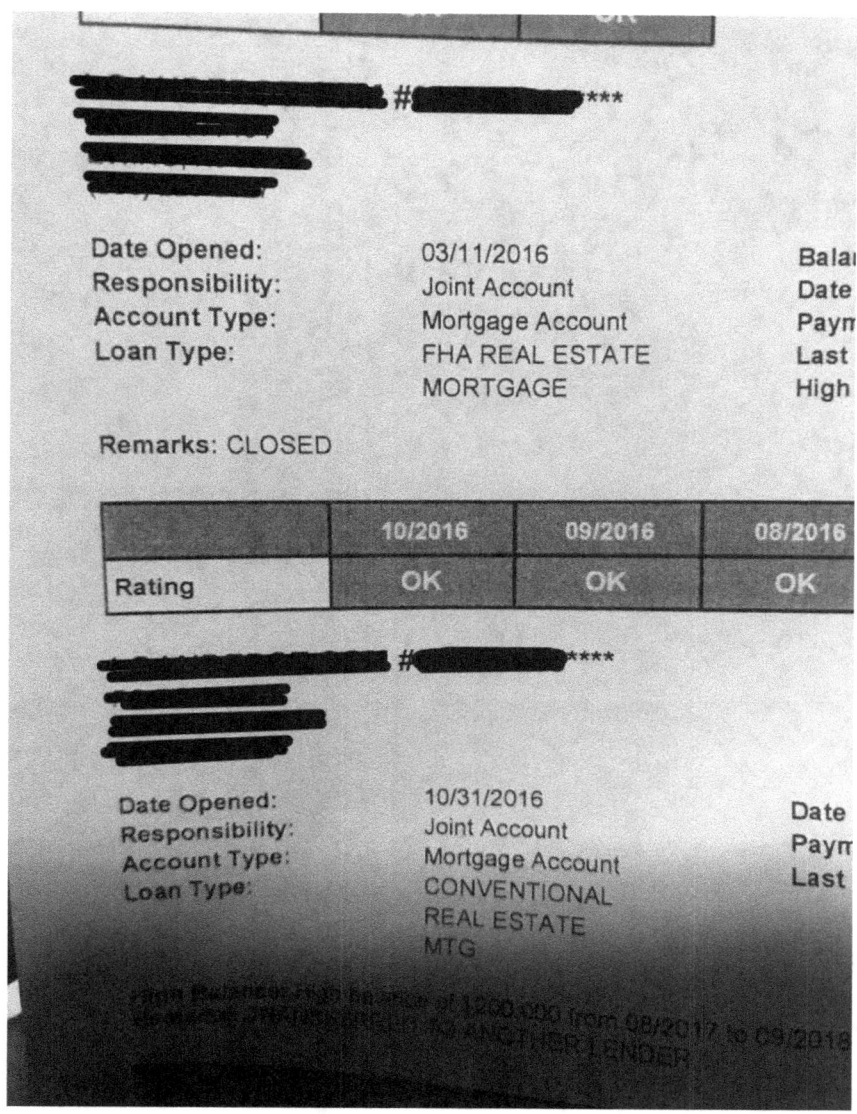

Figure 9-5: When did our account officially open for our home?
- 3/11/16. When did the account open after the whole process of
refinancing from FHA to Conventional to get out of that PMI
the same year? - 10/31/16

Figure 9-6 and Figure 9-7: My parents each having
fun on our 3-wheeler

Figure 9-8: Me having a blast on the 3-wheeler

Figure 9-9: My brother turning up some mud. I know we should be wearing helmets but hey, we rode these things in the 80's and early 90's, times were a little different

Figure 9-10: My father in a newspaper ad back in the 1980's

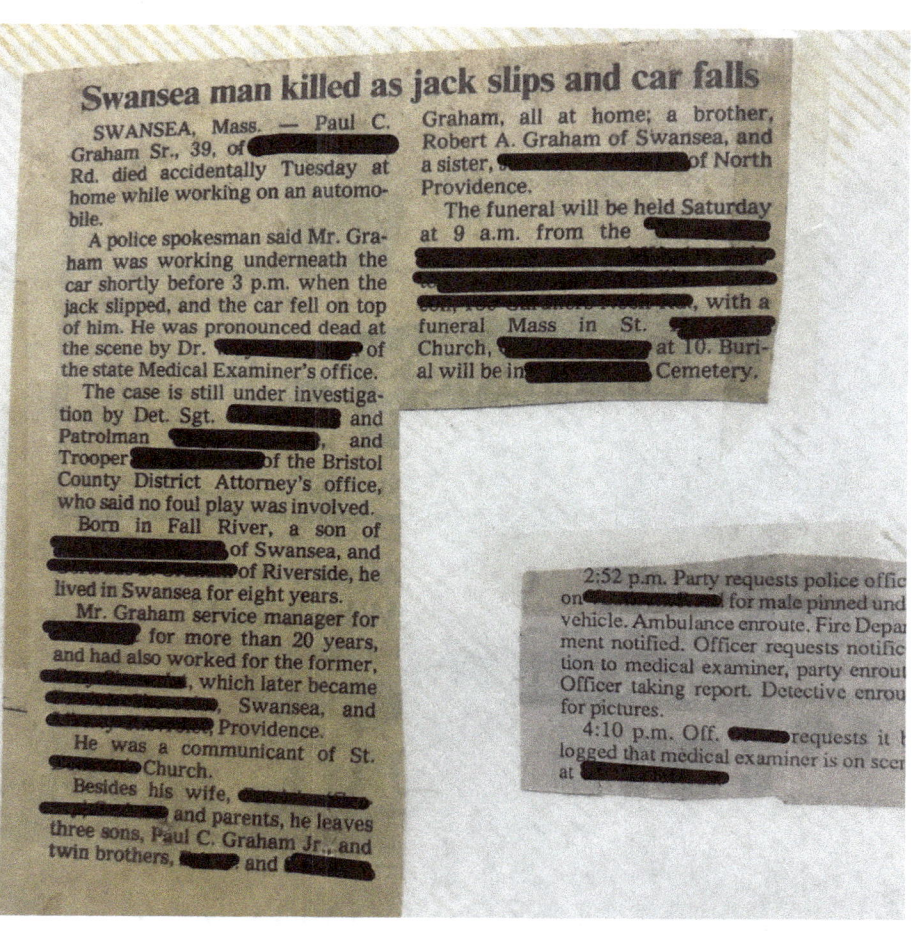

Swansea man killed as jack slips and car falls

SWANSEA, Mass. — Paul C. Graham Sr., 39, of ▨▨▨▨▨ Rd. died accidentally Tuesday at home while working on an automobile.

A police spokesman said Mr. Graham was working underneath the car shortly before 3 p.m. when the jack slipped, and the car fell on top of him. He was pronounced dead at the scene by Dr. ▨▨▨▨▨ of the state Medical Examiner's office.

The case is still under investigation by Det. Sgt. ▨▨▨▨▨ and Patrolman ▨▨▨▨▨, and Trooper ▨▨▨▨▨ of the Bristol County District Attorney's office, who said no foul play was involved.

Born in Fall River, a son of ▨▨▨▨▨ of Swansea, and ▨▨▨▨▨ of Riverside, he lived in Swansea for eight years.

Mr. Graham service manager for ▨▨▨▨▨ for more than 20 years, and had also worked for the former, ▨▨▨▨▨, which later became ▨▨▨▨▨, Swansea, and ▨▨▨▨▨ Providence.

He was a communicant of St. ▨▨▨▨▨ Church.

Besides his wife, ▨▨▨▨▨ and parents, he leaves three sons, Paul C. Graham Jr., and twin brothers, ▨▨▨▨▨ and ▨▨▨▨▨

Graham, all at home; a brother, Robert A. Graham of Swansea, and a sister, ▨▨▨▨▨ of North Providence.

The funeral will be held Saturday at 9 a.m. from the ▨▨▨▨▨ ▨▨▨▨▨, with a funeral Mass in St. ▨▨▨▨▨ Church, ▨▨▨▨▨ at 10. Burial will be in ▨▨▨▨▨ Cemetery.

2:52 p.m. Party requests police offic on ▨▨▨▨▨ for male pinned und vehicle. Ambulance enroute. Fire Depar ment notified. Officer requests notific tion to medical examiner, party enrout Officer taking report. Detective enrou for pictures.

4:10 p.m. Off. ▨▨▨▨▨ requests it logged that medical examiner is on scer at ▨▨▨▨▨

Figure 9-11: Newspaper clippings from my father's death

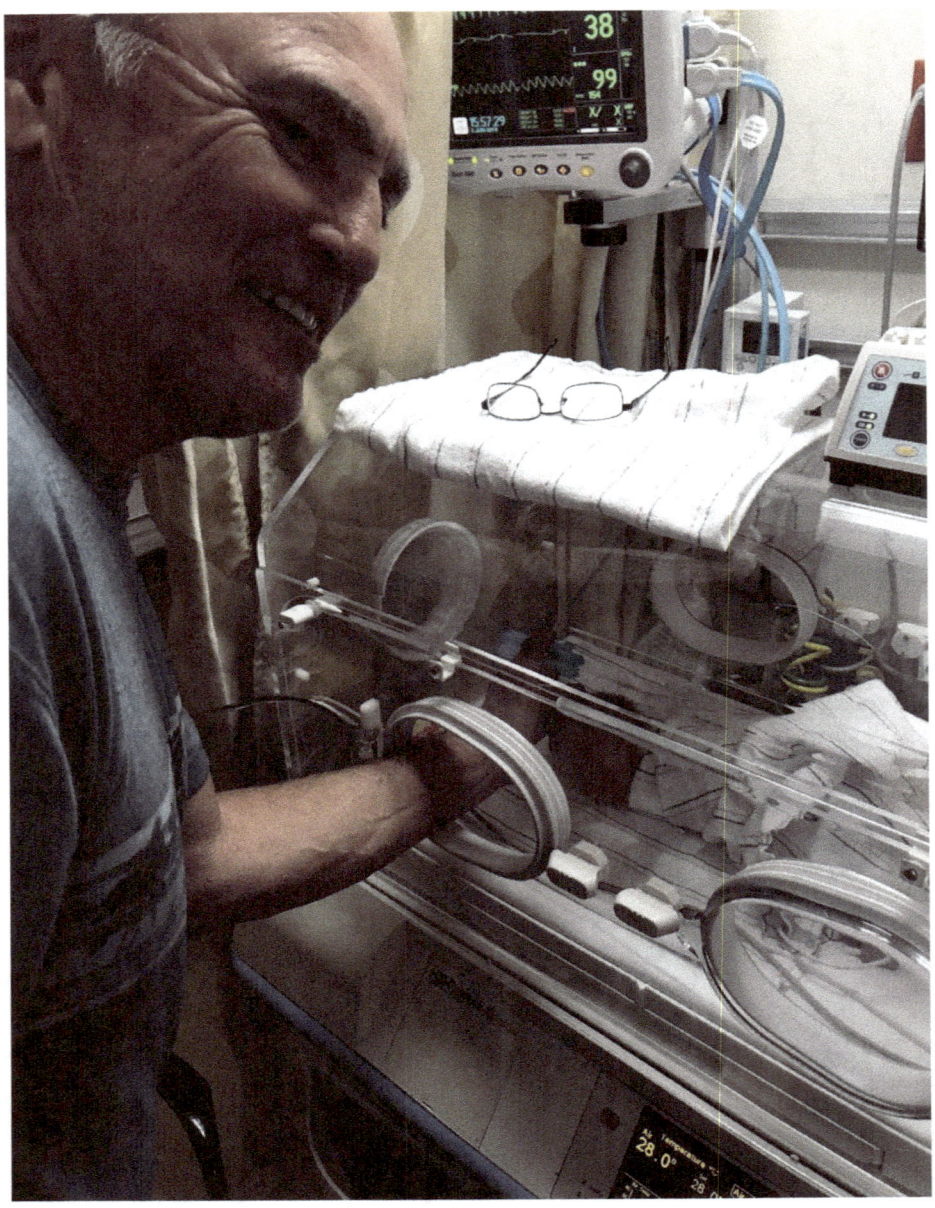

Figure 9-12: My Uncle Bob meeting one of my wife and I's miracles

Figure 9-13: Uncle Bob on the left and my Dad on the right, celebrating New Year's Eve after both had quit drinking alcohol. It wasn't always like this. They had some wild times in their early days. As time went on, the new stories weren't as crazy, but we really enjoyed moments like this – sometimes just relaxing, always having lots of laughs, but most importantly just spending time together enjoying the moment

Figure 9-14: My father taking my brothers and I to New England Dragway. Yeah, that's me - the cool kid in the sunglasses

Figure 9-15: My brothers and I

Figure 9-16: My hero

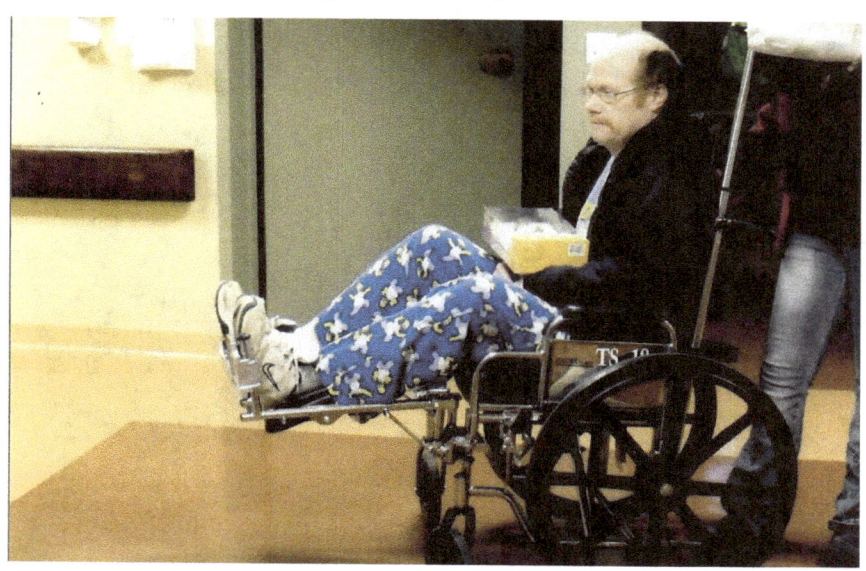

Figure 9-17: My father-in-law with the infamous "Jesus" doll that he played in the elevator

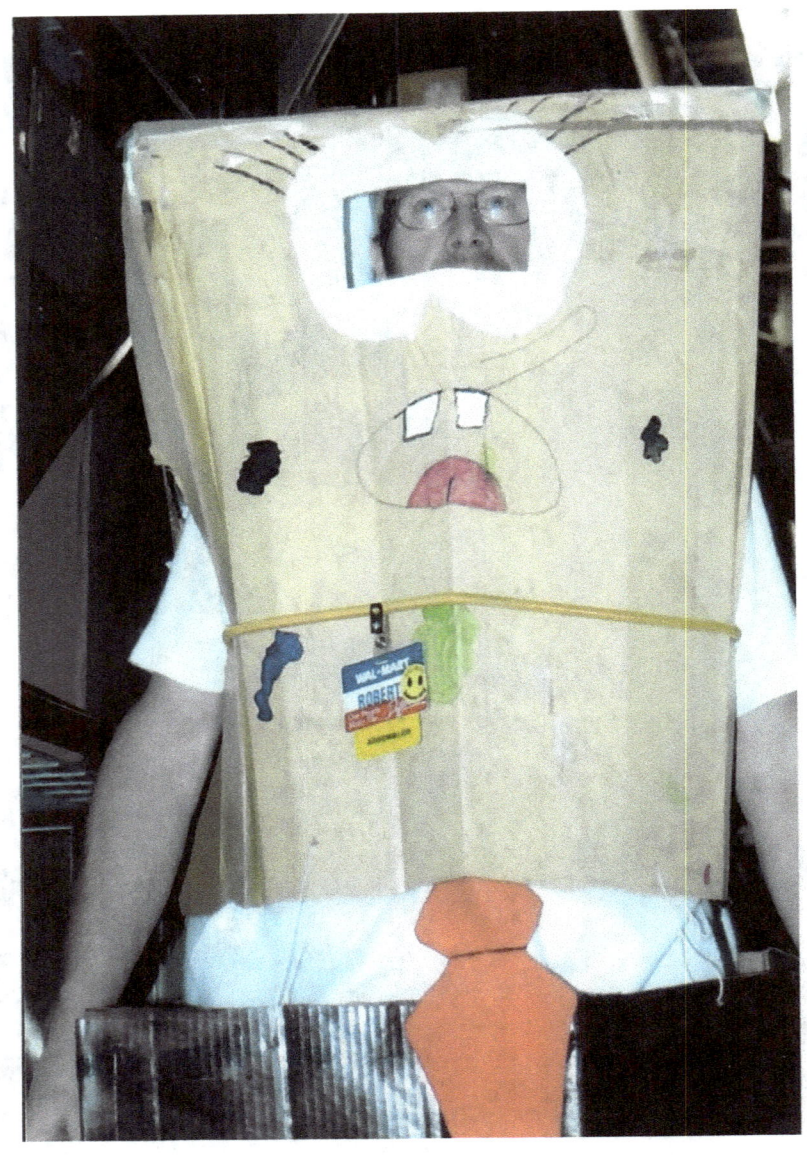

Figure 9-18: My father-in-law being his goofy self at Halloween

Figure 9-19: The early days of my wife and I, long before marriage – Our first roller coaster ride together!

Figure 9-20: My beautiful wife and I on our wedding day

Figure 9-21: My still and always beautiful wife and I at my bro-cuz's wedding. Photo by Amanda Lee's Captured Moments

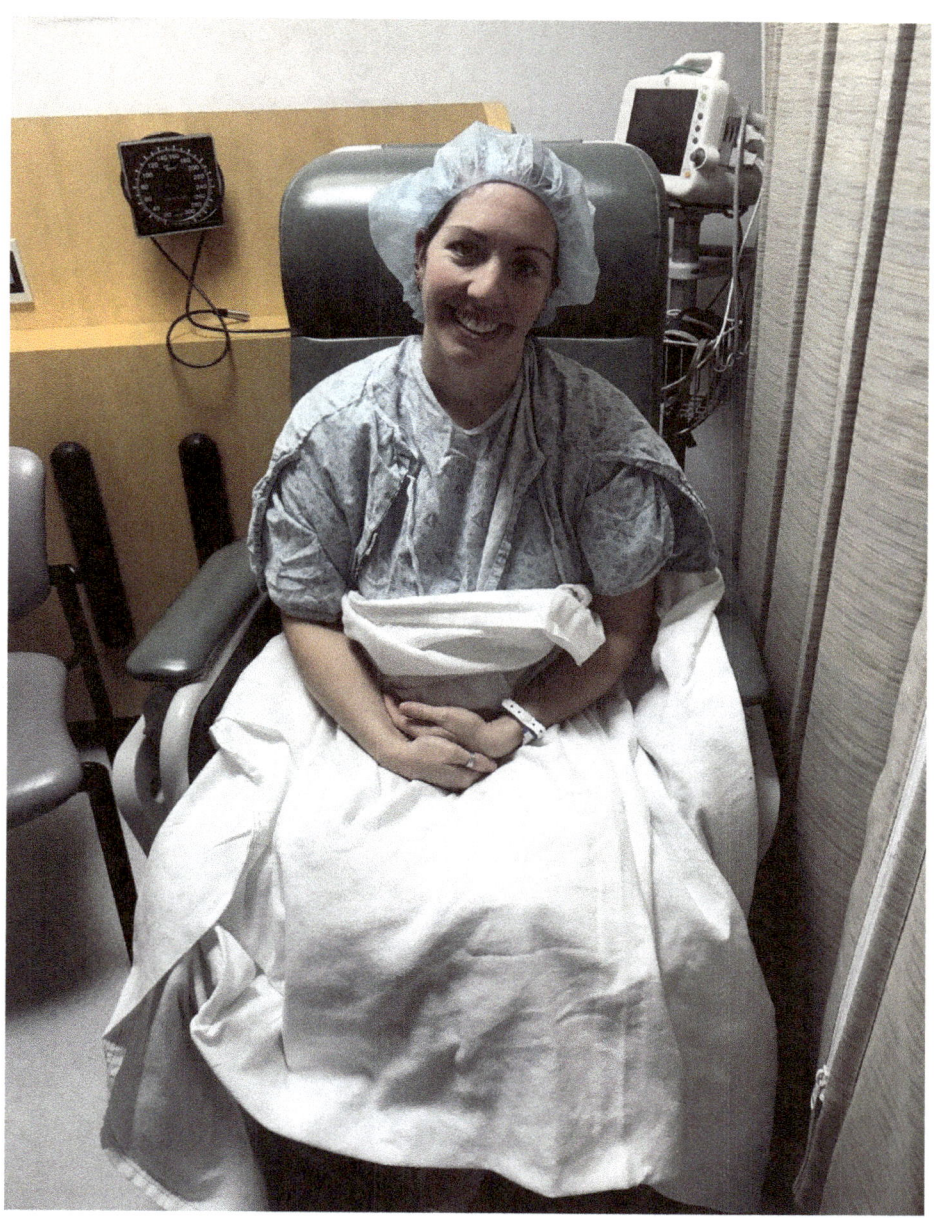

Figure 9-22: The day of the procedure that worked. Right after I told her "It's going to work this time"

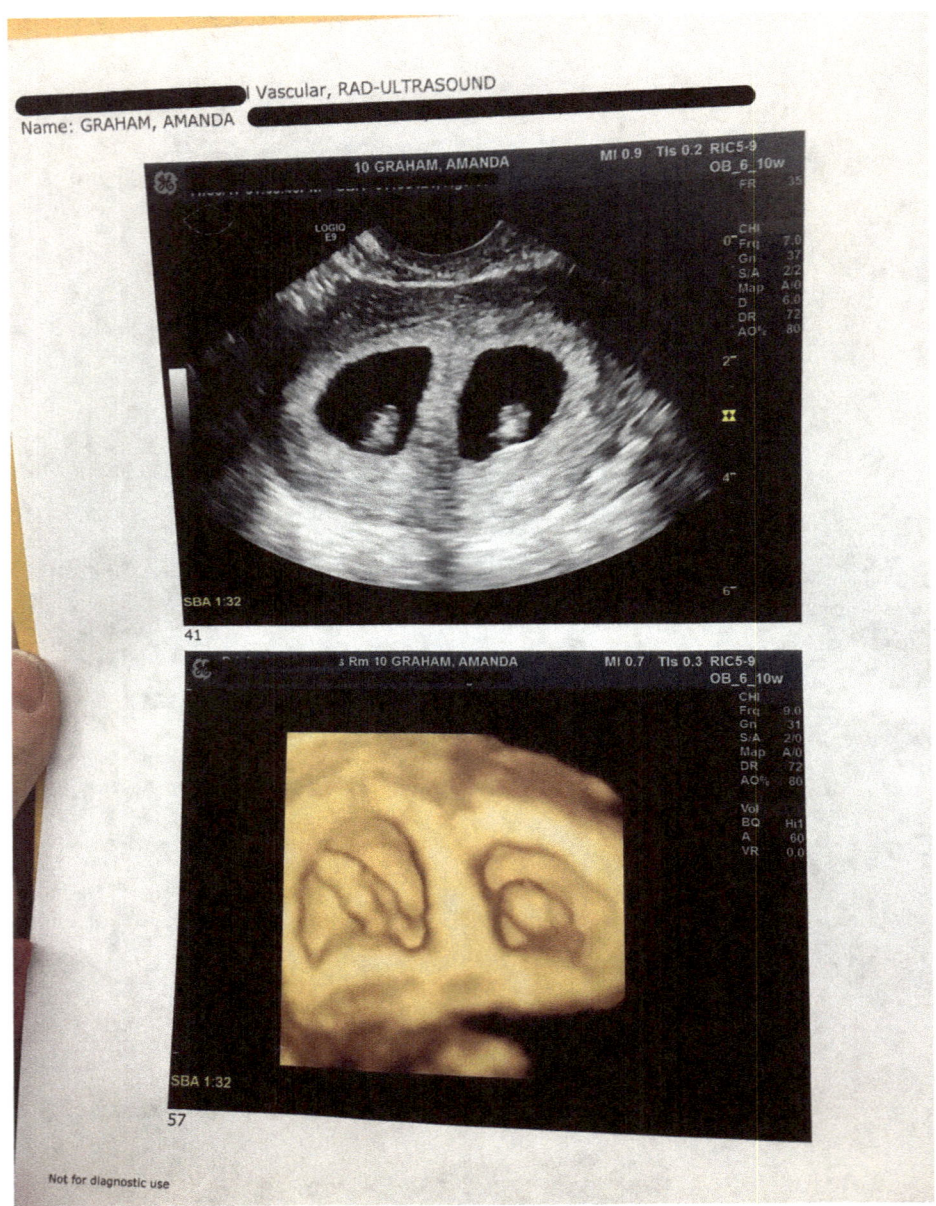

Figure 9-23: The first ultrasound images – Twins!

Figure 9-24: Our lives were now complete. Photo by Amanda Lee's Captured Moments

Figure 9-25: Our precious twins had arrived. Photo by Amanda Lee's Captured Moments

Thank you!

Thank you so much for taking the time to read my book. I truly do appreciate you using your greatest gift of time on this. I hope that you walk away feeling like maybe, just maybe there is some greater power out there. Maybe that power is GOD, the creator. If you enjoyed this book, I'd love for you to take the time to leave a review and encourage other readers to give it a chance. Maybe you or someone out there is struggling with some of the things that I struggled with in this book. Sometimes it's good to just know that someone else has gone through something similar. Maybe you have seen some signs in your life of something greater out there. Something that defies logic and science. I'd love to hear about them! Share your story with others in the comments and reviews for this book. Or feel free to reach out to me and tell me about it! My email is paulgrahamJR316@gmail.com. If it is something private that you don't want to share with everyone, that's ok too. I know all about that as I kept things hidden inside for decades and thought I may never tell anyone. Thank you for giving me the opportunity to tell my story!

www.ingramcontent.com/pod-product-compliance
Lightning Source LLC
Chambersburg PA
CBHW060527130626
46553CB00002B/680